# The Brief Sun

## A novel by

## Robert Ambros

ISBN: 0-7596-9292-0 (e-book)
ISBN: 0-7596-9293-9 (Paperback)

This book is printed on acid free paper.

1stBooks - rev. 8/5/02

*To my family*

# Chapter One

A Soviet labor camp in Northern Siberia
November 1941

We went to bed hungry, the day the conveyer gear in our wood processing plant shattered. We couldn't process the wood and as a result, none of us received our bread card. No processed wood, no bread card; that was the rule.

The reason for the breakdown was irrelevant to the guards. They'd claim we broke the conveyer on purpose, just to avoid work. But we gathered around the pieces of the broken gear as though we had lost a loved one. The camp, of course, didn't have a spare part. We had to find a solution.

I didn't realize the significance of losing bread rations when I first came to the labor camp. But I was only sixteen years old then, and after a year I understood it all too well.

Stefan had taught me how to survive. He was in his mid-thirties, and seemed to cope with things better than anyone. He'd been a carpenter before being deported to a labor camp just east of the Ural Mountains. They'd transferred him to this camp without explanation just prior to my arrival.

Stefan taught me that the bread rations were the key to survival. The bread was given out in the evening in six-, nine-, or twelve-ounce rations depending on the work done for the day. For breakfast and lunch, we only got stew and makusz. The stew consisted of black cabbage in water, sometimes fish heads, radishes, and rarely carrots; it had little nutritional value. Makusz was imitation oatmeal composed mostly of chopped grass. It didn't give you strength, Stefan told me, but it filled the stomach in the morning and kept away the hunger pains.

He also taught me about the death spiral. Missing one night's bread ration was no problem for all but the most severely sick. The weakness started for most after missing two days' ration of bread. With the weakness came less ability to work and subsequently, lower production. The less you produced, the smaller your ration. That was how most died; they entered the spiral. If someone was too far down the spiral, you couldn't save him no matter how much food you gave him. So that night, it was very simple. If we fixed the conveyer, we could process wood. If we processed enough wood, we could eat. We ate; we lived.

We spent the entire evening in the barrack discussing what to do. Patryk, a man in his mid-twenties from Lwow, proposed we go directly to the camp commandant and explain that the situation was simply hopeless; we needed a new part to process wood. But the others rejected the idea, claiming that we would never get to see him, or that he would tell us that there was no parts factory within a thousand miles. "There are engineers amongst yourselves. You must learn to help one another," he would tell us. So we went to sleep not knowing what to do.

That night was cold, but not too bad—about minus ten degrees centigrade. We'd tried to seal most cracks in the walls of our wooden barrack with mud the summer before, but an awful draft found its way through, most nights. The fire in our stove, fed with only the smallest scraps of wood, had died long ago. I wasn't sure why the guards didn't let us bring in more wood for the night. Some of the prisoners claimed the guards feared that we'd build wooden weapons from larger pieces. Little did the guards know that some of the men made weapons, but they were metal, not wooden. The guards had no reason to fear our firewood.

I tried to forget about the gear and get some sleep, but a dim light went on, followed by a growing commotion. I saw Stefan standing near my bunk.

"What's going on?" I asked.

"Kaz is on to something," he said.

"What?"

"Kaz is building a gear."

I raised my head and saw a small crowd had gathered around Kaz, seated under the dim lamp.

"Is that cast iron?" Jozef asked Kaz. "If that's cast iron, it won't take the strain."

Jozef was tall and thin with some gray in his beard. He had the army in his blood and couldn't shake off the defeat to the Germans back in 1939. He had been a lieutenant in the Polish Army when the war broke out. His battalion was destroyed fighting the Germans and he returned home to eastern Poland, which had been invaded by the Soviets a few weeks later. Two months after the Soviet invasion, he was arrested by the Soviet Secret Police—the NKVD—and sent to this camp. Whenever someone said the Soviets had stabbed us in the back, Jozef quickly pointed out that we'd been stabbed from all sides.

"Would I be filing cast iron?" asked Kaz. "I know what I'm doing."

"Where did you get the gear from?" asked Tomek.

"You know, I was lying there, and the idea just hit me," said Kaz. "I found this broken hand drill last summer in the mill. Don't ask me what I was going to do with it."

"You think it will fit?" asked Tomek.

"But then I just remembered it had a gear," said Kaz, ignoring the question. "A gear to turn the drill."

Kaz thinned the teeth of the gear with a small file someone had stolen from the tool shop.

"You didn't hide that drill under the window, did you? Tomek asked. "I got in trouble a couple of months ago, with that knife."

"I told you a hundred times, I had nothing to do with that knife," said Kaz.

Tomek rolled his eyes. He got the guardhouse once when they found a homemade knife right next to his bunk. He still thought Kaz had hidden it.

"The teeth look too wide," said Tomek.

"I'll make the son of a bitch fit, don't you worry about that."

My buddy Kaz—his real name was Kazimierz—had a deep voice, which made you forget how short he was. He claimed he didn't mind being short; short guys get the girls, he always said. Some men didn't understand his humor, didn't realize how funny he was. When he claimed he would become the commandant of this camp someday if he worked hard enough, some of the men called him crazy. Kaz was about twenty, a few years older than me.

The men said I was the youngest prisoner in the camp. Most were in their twenties and thirties; the older men died off. I was beardless and stood out amongst the other prisoners in the camp. My lips weren't cracked from scurvy yet.

They told me that it was very unusual for a sixteen-year-old to be sent to a labor camp for men. "You're tall, but your baby face gives you away," they said. "Why aren't you with your mother?" Most of the time, if you were under eighteen years old, they let you stay with your mother.

"NKVD must have an agenda against your father," they said. When I told them my father was an officer retired from the Polish Army, they nodded and said, "There it is." I didn't know why the Soviets would have had an agenda against my father. He was spending his time reading and fishing when the war broke out.

Yuriy bent over and examined the gear in detail. Yuriy was a Ukrainian by nationality but his family lived in Poland before deportation. "Don't file it down too much," he said. "You can make it smaller, but not bigger."

"He's right," agreed Tomek. Tomek and Jozef were both soldiers, but that was the only thing they had in common. Tomek was quick to complain and I never saw him solve a

4

problem. He was thin but the skin hung off his head; I suspected he was once quite fat.

Kaz pretended not to hear. "I know, I know," he finally said. "I didn't get to my current position in life without knowing what I'm doing."

Reveille sounded; it was five a.m. The sun would not come out for another five hours; the narrow streaks of light from the searchlights in the towers still cut across the dark sky. Of the fifty men in our barrack, ten of us worked in one of the camp's wood processing plants. We adjusted the rags on our feet and put on our canvas boots and pulled on the cloth coats we'd used as blankets. Our hats and gloves went on.

Those who didn't work in our plant asked about the commotion during the night. Some men munched on bread skins they'd saved from the night before.

The guard entered, a local Siberian named Rostovich. The locals were often meaner than the guards from western Russia. He wore a sheepskin coat, leather boots, and a hat made of real fur. He was overweight and spoke slowly, but his eyes prowled constantly.

"Up, up, and out," he mumbled.

Men slowly headed toward the door. Rostovich scanned the barrack, looking for anyone who did not rise, for those too sick to work, or those who were heading down the spiral. Rostovich knew who would be dead in a few days. He would not offer them food or medical care. He would only ask them if they wanted to rest that day. They would nod and he would leave them alone. For those claiming to be ill, he would offer them a trip to the infirmary but remind them that if the doctor turned them away, they would lose their bread ration and possibly earn a trip to the guardhouse.

Two prisoners remained in bed; they were both going down the spiral.

We lined up to be counted in the open space between the barracks and the main gate. The camp was rectangular and enclosed by a twelve-foot wooden fence with barbed wire on either side. Machine guns and searchlights were mounted in the watchtowers on each corner, and lamps midway between each tower went on with reveille. Ten prisoner barracks, two sets of five lined up parallel to each other, were separated from the planning office, the guard quarters, storehouses, kitchen, infirmary, tool shop, and a series of wood processing plants by barbed wire.

It was dark and cold and the monotonous counting only added to the gloom. I stood there half asleep until I remembered the gear concealed in Kaz's foot rags. Stefan had the file hidden in the rim of his hat. We would be searched after the count. If they found the gear and file, the guards would not be satisfied with the explanation that we were attempting to fix the conveyer belt. Stefan and Kaz would get the guardhouse for possessing "illegal instruments."

We should never have had Stefan and Kaz hide the instruments, I realized as we lined up to be searched. They were the only craftsmen among us; if they were held in detention, we would have no chance of fixing the conveyer. We would starve.

We stood in lines two abreast as two guards did the searching. Kaz and Stefan were ahead of me. As they moved closer and closer to the guards, my heart started to beat faster. I tried to look uninterested, but I imagined that my pounding heartbeat would give us away. The guards would hear it from where they stood and, suspicious, search Kaz and Stefan thoroughly. Snow squeaked as I shifted my feet; I wanted to run, but there was nowhere to go.

"If there is no rice, then they have to sell us bread at a discount," I heard one guard say to the other. He reached toward Kaz. I held my breath.

The other guard shook his head. "They said there will be no discount."

"Said who?" The guard patted his gloved hands over Kaz's chest, then waved him on.

Relief sent my pent breath gusting into the frigid air as twin puffs of steam. But now Stefan stepped up to the guard.

The guard didn't even look at Stefan. He patted Stefan's chest, still distracted by his conversation with the other guard. "Last winter, when they ran out of rice, we got the bread at half price." He jerked his head, signaling Stefan should move on.

My knees felt wobbly as we marched to the kitchen to the accompaniment of the guards' eternal song: "A step to the right, a step to the left, will be considered an attempt to escape." I wondered how Kaz's and Stefan's knees felt.

Clouds of steam billowed from the kitchen windows. We entered the welcome warmth of the mess hall, into air redolent with the smell of fish and garbage and the unwashed bodies of too many men. They were serving fish head stew today but as usual, it was mostly broth.

Yuriy once said that he found it very hard to believe someone was delivering fish heads to the camp. The cooks and guards stole the fish and left us with the scraps, of course. Nevertheless, Stefan had taught me never to waste a drop. "Forget the taste, it's your life," he said.

The guards rushed us through the meal. Another squad waited at the door to sit down and eat.

We whispered anxiously to one another as we headed to the wood processing plant, a plain wooden building housing a circular saw powered by an ancient steam engine that must have been built during the time of the Tsar. Kaz had gotten the gear past the guards, but would it run the conveyer?

A stack of logs waited outside the building, logs that should have been processed the day before. The tree cutters and log transporters, unlike us, had continued doing their job yesterday, and received their bread cards.

Kuzkhov and Bedchenko, the guards who met us at the plant door, were not the worst in the camp. Still, my hands curled in silent frustration when they started their routine.

"What are all these logs doing here?" asked Bedchenko, pointing at the stack. "Are you building a recreation center for yourselves?"

Most of the men looked away and pretended they didn't hear the remark—all except Jozef, who gave them a stare. It was difficult for an officer like Jozef, who'd had men under his command, to wear prison clothes and take orders from the Russian guards, particularly since he possessed a stubborn streak. He obeyed the guards, but they knew he was an officer and could smell his resentment.

"Don't you remember, comrade?" asked Kuzkhov. "They are pretending the conveyer is broken."

"Ah, yes, I remember," Bedchenko replied. "Vlad, do you know what I suspect? I suspect that when they get hungry enough, the conveyer will magically start working again."

Kuzkhov nodded. "I tend to agree with you; bread is a great motivator for the lazy."

"You know the gearbox is broken," said Jozef. "You saw the broken pieces yourself."

Jozef spoke Russian well. It was important, however, not to speak Russian too well. Russians were very suspicious of foreigners too fluent in their language. I spoke Russian poorly, and I almost never spoke to the guards.

Bedchenko unlocked the door to the plant. "Broken gears, broken belts, problems with the engine, you always have an excuse," he said. "Is that how you fought the Germans on the front, with excuses?"

"Let's see how well you fight them," Jozef snapped.

Bedchenko laughed. "You worry about your bread card and not what we do with the Germans," he said.

Kuzkhov, on the other hand, was not amused. "The Germans will be just as pleased they entered Russian soil as you were," he said.

"It's very simple," said Bedchenko. "Find a way to cut that wood, and we'll give you a bread card."

"If the camp had the spare parts you so obviously need, we wouldn't be down," said Jozef.

"You may put your complaints in writing and submit them to the commandant," said Bedchenko quite seriously, then laughed as he and Kuzkhov opened the doors to the plant.

We gathered around Kaz as he examined the machinery to see if the new gear would fit.

"The hole's too small, but the teeth look good," he said.

Kaz had been studying to be a craftsman when the war broke out. His story was similar to mine—we were from the same province and our fathers were both retired servicemen. Most of our stories were the same, with only variations on the theme. There were some non-Poles in the camp; in one barrack there were a few Estonians and Ukrainians, even an American, I heard, but most of us were Polish prisoners. Following the Soviet invasion of a free and independent Poland two years ago, the Soviets had deported us from our homes in Eastern Poland. Our crime was living on our land and we were now being punished for "our crimes against the peaceful Soviet people."

The NKVD came for my father and Kaz's in the fall of 1939 and took them away without explanation. They returned and arrested the remaining members of our families in February of the next year.

"Evenly," said Stefan to Kaz. "Keep the hole round; alternate your strokes."

Kaz ignored the others, but he would listen to Stefan. Everyone knew Stefan was a skilled craftsman. I liked to watch Stefan work; every movement he made had a purpose. He moved so quickly and efficiently, you didn't even notice his limp. I didn't know what was wrong with his leg, but the limp had kept him out of the army in 1939.

"Work it diagonally so you don't create a crevice," added Tomek.

Jozef shook his head. "He knows what he's doing," he said. "He's doing the job, just let him do it."

"Jozef's right," said Yuriy. "Come on, Andrzej, let's get the stove going."

Yuriy and I gathered wood scraps to light the stove. At Patryk's suggestion, the others chopped wood with small ax blades, building up a supply of fragments to keep the stove going. Tomek didn't help. He kept looking over Kaz's shoulder.

Jobs in the plant were rotated. This month, Stefan and I pulled logs onto the belt for Jozef and Tomek, who did the sawing. Kaz and Yuriy sorted the cut wood and Patryk and Mr. Rakowski transported the cut wood to storage. You would think prisoners who had come here from the universities would find the physical labor onerous, but this was not true of Patryk. He was not much bigger than Kaz, but he got the work done—unlike Tomek, who frequently hindered our efforts to meet the quota.

The next month, all of us would be outside cutting the trees down and a different squad would work the plant. Cutting down trees was the worst job in the winter. Although none of us had spoken of it yet, we knew Mr. Rakowski, who was in his late fifties, would not survive a month in the deadly wind. He had to find a way to stay indoors during the winter, or he would perish.

I stepped outside with an armload of kindling and glanced at the sun, barely above the horizon. It was about ten a.m. Here, the sun arced low across the sky, never rising over our heads before it set, only a few hours later. Sometimes I thought it made its brief appearance just to remind us it was still there.

I turned away to stack the kindling against the building, and the memories came flooding back.

On a working Sunday last spring, I'd stood here with wood in my hands, overcome by the horror of what I'd been through. I had only been in the camp about two months. My God, I thought, what terrible thing had I done to deserve this?

I had no idea where my family was. First they'd taken my father away, then they came for the rest of us. They sent six-year-old Michal away with my mother. I didn't know where they'd sent my older brother, Stan. I'd been stacking wood that Sunday evening when the questions all hit me at once. Were

10

they all in Siberia? How would I find them? How would I get home?

I'd dropped to my knees and started to cry. I had not known that such terrible things could happen. I screamed inwardly, *My God, where are you?* The men in my squad saw me cry. They glanced outside as they walked by the door, but no one said anything to me; they pretended it did not happen.

That night in the barrack, Stefan bent down beside my bunk and whispered, "Andrzej, remember what the camp commandant told us the day we got here, that we were sent to spend the rest of our lives here and we'll never leave?"

I nodded.

"It's bullshit," he said. "You listen to us, Andrzej. Do what they tell you to do. Keep quiet. Don't talk to anyone you don't know well. We'll get you out of here. I promise."

I nodded and turned over. I swore to myself that I would never break down again.

"No," I said now, as if reaffirming that vow. I forced the word through clenched teeth, and stacked the kindling poorly in my haste to get back inside, away from this spot and its memories. "I'll get through this," I said, as I had every time I'd stood here since that first time. "They won't break me."

Inside, Kaz had enlarged the hole enough that the gear slipped onto the bar, but the teeth still needed to fit better. He put his file back to work. In less than an hour, he signaled to Stefan, who turned on the conveyer.

The wheel turned; the belt moved. Kaz raised his arms in triumph.

"We'll never cut all these logs in time," said Tomek.

Stefan walked up and closely examined the gear.

"What's wrong?" asked Kaz.

"Nothing," he said. "Let's see how long it will last."

"We'll know when a few logs pass," said Tomek.

Stefan shook his head. "It'll take longer than that."

We got to work. Stefan and I started to load the logs. Stefan took his work very seriously, even something as simple as

11

loading logs onto a conveyer belt. "Why don't you think?" he yelled when one slipped from my numb hands.

I didn't pay much attention when he yelled; I received more abuse from my older brother Stan, and I knew Stefan got emotional sometimes. I'd seen him get emotional once when someone asked him about his two daughters, and I knew I should never bring up that subject.

The gear held as the first logs went through. Everyone started to work with extra vigor—everyone except frail Mr. Rakowski. He'd never actually shown interest in the new gear. I once overheard Jozef tell Stefan that Mr. Rakowski had given up. When Mr. Rakowski came up here, Stefan had told me, he'd had most of his hair. In less than a year, he'd become almost completely bald.

Back home, he'd been an accountant, nearing retirement. He and his wife and five children had been arrested, but he didn't know what had happened to his family. I felt a strange sorrow for him. Back home, Mr. Rakowski would have been an authority figure to me, held in the same esteem as my father or my schoolmaster, or our family priest. But here, he was a beaten man. I never talked to him; I didn't know what to say. Some of the men gave him portions of their bread when he was too weak to work; I never did. For some strange reason, I would have been ashamed to.

The authority figures here were so different from those at home. Even when I was angry with my schoolmaster or my priest for being strict with me, I knew deep inside that they were doing it for my own good. But to the guards, I was an animal present only to perform a certain function. If I was able to do the job, they fed me. If not, they'd let me die. It happened all the time.

At first, I thought the guards despised me because I was a foreigner, a Pole. But with time, I realized they treated everyone like animals, even their own people.

We cut wood all day and cleared the pile. But at the end of the day Stefan looked at the machinery and announced, "The gear's cracking. It's giving all it's got, but the strain is too much. It wasn't designed for this."

Kaz ran up and stared at the gear. "Shit, all for nothing."

Patryk raised his arms in resignation. "Go to the commandant," he said. "Tell him it's useless, we simply need a new part."

"How much longer will it hold?" asked Jozef.

Stefan shrugged. "A minute, a week—impossible to say."

It had served its purpose, at least for one day—I received my black bread and devoured every last crumb. When we got back to the barrack, Stefan and Jozef agreed to try to see the commandant about the gear. But talk quickly turned to what Kaszynski had heard.

I didn't know Kaszynski well, but I knew he had a good nose for news. He had been working in the tool shop earlier in the day and overheard two guards talking. He claimed he heard one guard tell the other there was to be some sort of resettlement.

Stefan jumped out of his bunk. "Resettlement?" he asked sharply. "Do you know any more, like who or when?"

"What's resettlement?" I asked, looking quickly between Kaszynski and Stefan.

"You don't want to know, Andrzej," said Stefan, but his eyes stayed on Kaszynski.

"That's all I could make out," said Kaszynski. "But the guards themselves seemed concerned."

"Who were the guards?"

"Kutuzov and some other guy I didn't recognize," said Kaszynski.

"Resettlement in winter?" Tomek exclaimed. "That's crazy."

"Who brought up resettlement, Kutuzov or the other one?" Stefan asked Kaszynski.

"Kutuzov was the one who did all the talking. He was the one that looked worried."

"Kutuzov knows what's going on," said Stefan. He suddenly remembered my question and turned to me. "When they want to make room in a camp, they move out the prisoners and make them build a new camp. They move everyone out to an empty field in the middle of nowhere and surround the area with barbed wire so no one will escape. You then start to build. Not your barracks, of course, but the camp walls, then the commandant's quarters, the guard quarters, and everything else."

"Just pray there are good engineers and builders among you," said Tomek.

"When they are satisfied," Stefan continued, "they will let you build your own barracks. In the meantime, you live outside like you did on our trip up here from Surgut. A Russian prisoner in my old camp told me he had never seen anyone over the age of thirty survive a resettlement in the winter."

I hoped I never had to repeat a trip like the one from the train station to the camp. There were no train tracks near the camp. The trains that brought us to Siberia took us as far as the town of Surgut, and we walked from there. It was still winter, and there'd been a foot or two of snow on the ground. For ten days, we marched night and day, chained together, with guards at our sides and in the trucks that led the way. During rest periods, we built a snow bank to protect us from the wind and lit a fire in the center of the sheltered area. After marching for several days, I became so exhausted that I didn't care if I lived or died. My mind gave up, but by some miracle, my legs kept moving.

"You don't know if that's the case," Patryk said, rising from his bunk. "They could have been talking about anything."

"You heard Kaszynski," said Stefan. "The guards were worried. They don't like resettlement either."

Patryk was not convinced. "Why do they need more room for prisoners? No more than usual have been coming up."

"It's a big country," said Jozef. "Just because we haven't seen more prisoners doesn't mean anything."

"They could be making room for German POWs," said Tomek. "The Russians have been fighting the Germans for months now."

Jozef shook his head. "No way. The Russians shoot German soldiers on sight."

Jozef loved to correct others. He was very sure of himself and knowledgeable of world events and politics. Patryk was educated too, but Jozef was ten years older and had more experience to draw on. When someone told him that the Soviets should have granted him the rights of a POW, he pointed out that the Soviet Union had never signed the Geneva Convention. He was by far the most patriotic of us all. Patryk said Jozef's teachers must have been nationalists.

"Maybe the Russians are winning and pushing the Germans out of Poland," said Yuriy. "The Russians may be deporting more Poles, this time from western Poland."

"That, I wouldn't put past them," said Jozef. "But we have no idea what the German-Russian front looks like; not even the guards know."

Stefan lay back down on his bunk, saying, "There is nothing to do but wait and see what this is about. Better save some of your rations, fellows. Make sure you have extra rags. That's all you can do."

I was too tired to worry. I lay down in my bunk and fell asleep immediately.

\*\*\*

Much later, I woke in the darkness when someone gently tapped me on the shoulder. A hand covered my mouth. I tried to spring up, but I was pushed back.

"Andrzej, it's only us."

I recognized the voice: Stefan. I guessed that Jozef was with him.

"Can you hear me?" he whispered.

He felt me nod beneath his hand.

"Andrzej, don't say a word, just listen. Forget the gear, Andrzej; this winter resettlement thing is really bad. It can break even a very strong man. If there is going to be a resettlement, it's time we take action, and it has to be fast. They can send you off to a resettlement without notice, not even allowing you to collect your things.

"You know the reason we have not tried to escape, right? It's because the odds of surviving the trip are very poor. The closest place you can escape to is thousands of miles away— Mongolia or Afghanistan, maybe. But the odds of surviving a resettlement in winter are not much better. Remember, if we resettle, we'll all be separated. It takes time to determine if a man can be trusted. You could be dead before you have a chance to develop trust in anyone."

I relaxed and he removed his hand from my mouth. "You were lucky with us, Andrzej; we all get along. You may not be so lucky again. You may get stuck with thugs. If they are going to resettle us, we are leaving. We want you to come with us. There will be six of us. We think we have a way out. I once told you that we will get you out of here, remember? Well, this is it. Will you go?"

"I can't go to a foreign country," I whispered. "I have to find my family."

"You can't find your family if you're dead," whispered Jozef. "Tell us tomorrow if you want in. In the meantime, don't breathe a word of this to anyone."

"I won't," I murmured. They left and I rolled over. I didn't have to think it over until the next day. I had no choice but to go with them.

## Chapter Two

I dreamed of the trains again. This time, I dreamt I was looking for my father.

The trip from my hometown to Siberia seemed endless. I never saw anyone I knew on the trains. We switched trains several times, but each time the cattle cars were so packed that everyone had to stand. The only light in the car came from sunlight seeping in through small cracks in the walls. The cold draft came through those same holes. Men took turns standing in the middle of the car, where it was warmer. They fed us only once every day or two.

In my dream, I felt again the hunger tearing at my stomach; the icy air buffeting the backs of my legs, burning into my flesh, then numbing it when I was unable to move, even to turn around.

One night, someone kept leaning on me and I kept pushing him off. The next day, when they opened the car to feed us, I found out he was dead. He'd died standing up and remained upright, propped up by the people jammed in around him until the doors were opened. The guards dumped his body in the snow adjacent to the tracks, with the bodies of others—mostly elderly men—who had died since the last stop. They didn't even bury them.

When I got to the camp, the other prisoners told me the guards on the trains wanted the older men to die; they were under orders not to help them. The Soviets did not want to feed men who could not produce, once they got to the camp.

I dreamed I was looking through the cattle cars for my father when I suddenly saw him standing by the tracks. He spotted me and called me over. He told me he would wait here by the tracks for my younger brother, Michal, and my mother. He wanted me to get on the train and look for Stan. I wanted to ask him where we would meet, but it was too late—the train was leaving. I lost sight of him.

Reveille sounded. It was five a.m.

As I rose with the others to start the day, I knew my decision had not changed. I would go with Stefan and Jozef. I'd let them know in the processing plant; that would be the safest place.

Rostovich, the guard, entered and scanned the barrack. "Up, up, and out," he said.

As he'd opened the door, I saw all the lights on in the camp; that was unusual. The last time all the lights were on, they'd been looking for escapees. But things seemed orderly, this day. I didn't hear sirens and the guards were not running around with those dogs that scared the hell out of me.

Only one thing scared me more than those attack dogs, more than hunger: interrogation. The NKVD had interrogated some of the prisoners, mostly soldiers of the Polish Army, before they were sent up here. They tortured them for days and then forced them to sign phony confessions stating that they had been spying on the Soviet Union. Only after they signed were they allowed to leave the prison cells of the NKVD. Thank God I had never been interrogated.

Snow was falling as I left the barrack for the head count, but there was no wind; it was a bearable morning. I followed the others toward our usual space, but the guards directed us to gather with the other squads for a general announcement. This had never happened before. As long as I'd been in the camp, the head counts had never varied. I felt like I was breaking a long-standing habit as we moved toward the gathering crowd. I glanced at Stefan. It looked like resettlement after all.

The camp commandant strode across the empty space at the front of the gathered prisoners and stopped facing us, waiting as a guard announced his presence and called us to attention. I had seen the commandant only once before, on the day we arrived at the camp. I didn't even know his name. He was a short, fat man with a whiny voice.

The commandant read a statement from a piece of paper he held in his gloved hand: "Attention, prisoners! A decree by the Presidium of the Supreme Soviet of the Union of Soviet Socialist Republics grants a general amnesty to all Polish citizens imprisoned in the Soviet Union. The amnesty is extended to Polish military personnel. The amnesty is immediate and includes the prisoners of this camp. Amnestied prisoners will be issued papers of deportation. Amnestied prisoners may apply for permanent residency in the Soviet Union."

He paused, but kept his eyes on the paper he held. After a moment, he continued.

"Attention, Polish prisoners! The fascists of Germany have invaded your homeland. A Soviet-Polish agreement has been made for the formation of a Polish army in the territories of the Union of Soviet Socialist Republics. The army is being formed for the defense of your homeland. All amnestied prisoners may apply for enlistment. That is all." Still without looking at us, the commandant turned and strode quickly across the empty space in front of us. He hurried through the opening in the barbed wire perimeter and disappeared among the administrative buildings.

Everyone just stood there for a moment, even the guards. Then some prisoners started waving their hands in the air, and whooping.

My Russian was so poor, I didn't even understand what the commandant had said to us. Even more confused by the behavior of the whooping prisoners, I turned to Tomek, who stood next to me. "What did he say?"

"He said we are free."

"What?" I didn't believe him at first. He'd answered with no expression at all on his face. Surely, if it were true, he'd be as overjoyed as the other prisoners.

"They are letting us go," he said.

"Why?"

"They want us to fight the Germans."

I turned and looked at Jozef. He was staring into the air. I looked away, saw guards leaving their posts and gathering into groups. Prisoners were forming into groups, too. I saw Stefan talking to Yuriy. I looked around for a guard, ready to ask permission to join them, but the guard was gone. I slowly walked over.

"What if it's a trap?" Yuriy asked Stefan as I joined them. "What if they shoot us all when we start to leave and then claim we were trying to escape?"

"I was thinking the same thing," said Stefan.

"Bullshit! We're free!" yelled Kaz in joy.

"They wouldn't be issuing deportation papers if it was a trick," said Jozef.

Jozef thought it was for real? I hadn't expected this from him. He was usually the most suspicious of men. He was always suspicious of new prisoners who looked well fed. I'd heard him say the NKVD monitored us, even in this camp.

Kaz tried to grab Tomek and whirl him around, but Tomek brushed him off. I was still confused; I didn't know whether to celebrate or be suspicious. When I looked around again, I noticed others looking around too, seeking someone who knew what was going on. Some clown walked over to the main gate and told the guard to open the gate; he wanted to leave. The guard asked for his deportation papers and the man returned to the crowd.

Jozef spotted a man named Kalinski and walked over to him. Stefan turned to me. "Let's see if this is real, Andrzej," he said. "It could be, but let's make sure. The guards Kaszynski heard talking may have known something was going to happen, but not exactly what. They may have thought it was a resettlement."

"The guards must have been talking about *their* resettlement," Kaz quipped.

"Maybe, but they don't look like they knew about this," said Stefan as he looked around.

Some of the men started heading to their barracks unaccompanied by guards. It looked real to me—never before had I seen prisoners just wandering around. But I'd learned caution; I wouldn't let these people fool me. I stuck close to the others in my squad and stayed quiet.

Men started to walk in and out of the barracks freely. We finally returned to our own. The man Jozef had been speaking to, Kalinski, entered our barrack with a small group of men and headed right for Jozef. Some men rose from their bunks as he passed and followed him, curious. Kalinski was a very serious man and he looked like he had something important to announce. Even though he wore prisoner's clothes and had a gray beard, he carried himself like an important man. He reminded me of my schoolmaster.

As usual, Jozef rose when he saw Kalinski. "Find anything out?" Jozef asked.

"It's for real," declared Kalinski.

Jozef's eyes narrowed. "Are you sure?"

"The commandant's assistant showed me the decree, printed in the Communist newspaper."

Behind him, the men who had gathered to listen shouted with joy. I grinned at Kaz, who tried to lift Tomek; Tomek brushed him off.

Kalinski went on. "The decree was given in August."

Stefan's brows rose. "August? The news took three months to reach us?"

"It's possible the news took that long to get here," said Kalinski. "They may have been stalling us, maybe not."

"I bet you those bastards wanted to meet their quota," said Tomek. "They kept us here to meet their quota."

"What about the army?" asked Jozef, the soldier in him surfacing again.

"The army is forming in the south," Kalinski said.

"Where?"

Kalinski shrugged. "That is all they know. If you want to enlist, you have to make it to southern Russia."

"Stalin is panicking!" crowed Tomek, as if he'd really hit the nail on the head. "That's what this is all about! The Germans must be winning on the Eastern Front and Stalin is panicking.

He's getting desperate. He's even willing to let prisoners go. He must be desperate!"

"Yes, yes, you're right, Tomek." Jozef sat down slowly. "Southern Russia? They must be forming the army far east of the front, so they can train."

"Who wants to help the Russians fight the Germans?" asked Kaz. "They can all kill each other, for all I care."

"Kaz has a point," said Stefan, turning to Kalinski. "Who will control this army?"

"I imagine the Soviets will demand some control," said Kalinski. "But it is supposed to be a Polish army."

"And a way out of here!" yelled Yuriy. "A legitimate way!"

Everyone chuckled. Everyone agreed on that.

"How are they going to get us to the south?" asked Jozef. "Will they give us any provisions? Train tickets?"

"That is the least they can do," said Kaz.

"The short answer is, they will not help us in any way," said Kalinski. "The commandant said he had no money to give out and he is not authorized to issue train tickets."

"Bullshit," said Tomek. "They're screwing us again."

"And if you go outside," said Kalinski, "you'll notice the guards have surrounded the tool shop and the storehouses. It looks like they won't let us take a thing with us. Have any of you noticed the guards seem a little concerned about us?"

"Definitely," said Kaz. "They are afraid of us now, afraid of our numbers. I think they can't wait for us to leave."

"I think you're right," said Kalinski. "But I think we should maintain good relations with them. If the camp won't give us supplies, we'll need to barter with the guards."

"Very true," said Jozef.

The guards were reluctant to barter with us. They even shook their heads and walked away from a good watch offered in exchange for some bread. The guards' superiors considered it a bribe, and the penalty for accepting was stiff. I wondered if things were different, now that they were letting us go.

"Are they letting everyone leave?" asked Yuriy.

"Did they say when we could leave?" asked Jozef.

"They told me as early as tomorrow," said Kalinski. "They're working on the deportation papers right now." He grabbed Jozef's shoulder. "Looks like this is it, Jozef. Let's meet later and plan the trip." Then he and his men left.

"I don't want to go to southern Russia," I said. "I want to go southwest. I want to go home."

I didn't tell the others, but I didn't want to join any army. That was the last thing I wanted to do. My father had always talked about careers in the military for Stan and me, but I hadn't wanted to hear anything about it. My brother, of course, could think of nothing but entering the military academy.

"You go home now," said Jozef, "and you will find a Russian tank in your backyard and a German tank in your front yard."

"Jozef's right, Andrzej," said Stefan. "South is the only way out of here. You go in any direction but southern Russia and you will perish for sure. Besides, who but a Polish army will get us back to our homes?"

Stefan was starting to sound like Jozef, with this army talk.

"How the hell are we going to make it to southern Russia with no provisions and no transportation?" Tomek demanded. "You're talking about a couple of thousand miles."

There was silence; no one had an answer.

Jozef finally spoke. "The same way we came up. We'll have to go to Surgut on foot."

Tomek bent over as if in pain. "Not again," he said.

"From there, we'll have to find a way to make it to the Trans-Siberian Railway and go west. Once we're west of the Ural Mountains, we'll head south."

Kaz was optimistic. "So we have to walk to Surgut. We did it before, but this time we are going in the right direction." He turned his back to Tomek. "Don't worry buddy, I'll carry you on my back all the way. It's only a couple of hundred miles. You can even eat my food while I carry you."

A few laughed, but Tomek ignored Kaz and said, "They are sending us home to defend our homeland? What a crock of shit. What, they didn't know that Germany invaded Poland two years ago? Next they will be telling us they sent us here for our own protection. You know what I think? I think they are planning to use us as cannon fodder."

"They use everyone for cannon fodder, even their own, Tomek. You know that," said Jozef.

"At least we are going in the right direction," repeated Kaz.

As Tomek continued to criticize the Russians, it suddenly occurred to me that my dream from the night before was coming true. My father was telling me it was time for me to come home. *Tomorrow,* I thought, *I'll take my first steps outside of this camp in almost a year.* If going to southern Russia was the only way out, then so be it.

My father had also told me to find my brother Stan. Stan would be trying to find the army for sure. Maybe Stan had heard about the army earlier than I had, and was already with them. My father had been in the service; maybe they would use him as a special advisor. My mother? When she and little Michal got their deportation papers, they would have to go south also. That was what father must have been trying to tell me—he wanted me to find Stan while he sought mom and Michal. I had to go south to join them, but I didn't want to hear about joining this army.

\*\*\*

The barracks—the whole camp, for that matter—became chaotic. Camp personnel and prisoners ran constantly between barracks. Kaz exchanged six sewing needles for two loaves of bread. Tomek got a pound of real oatmeal for a small knife he'd made out of a hacksaw blade. When Kaz warned Tomek not to give away something he would need for the trip, and Tomek showed him four more knives. I exchanged my sole possession, my German watch, for a sack of potatoes and three strips of cloth. Jozef was trying to find someone with a map. Yuriy feared he would not get his deportation papers because he was of Ukrainian descent. Mr. Rakowski didn't want to leave at all, despite encouragement from the others.

Jozef handed me a piece of flint rock, a nail, and a bunch of grass roots and told me that those small items could mean the difference between life and death. Someone got two sacks of potatoes for a watch that was much cheaper than mine. A prisoner from another barrack entered and announced he'd exchange potatoes for rubles.

String was a popular item in the bartering. For the life of me, I didn't know why someone would want string. Stefan got four loaves of bread dipped in honey for a cigarette case; I hadn't even known there was honey in the camp.

In the midst of this, Kalinski and his pack entered our barrack and found Jozef. "The bartering, it's just like I said," said Kalinski.

Jozef just stared at him.

"We have to go over the trip to Surgut," said Kalinski.

"Have you been able to locate a map?" asked Jozef. "I've had no luck."

Kalinski waved away his concern. "There is one in the commandant's office, but they want one hundred rubles just to copy it. We can't come up with that. Now, how long ago did you come up?"

"About a year and a half ago," said Jozef.

"What do you remember about the direction?"

"Judging by the sun, northeast. We headed northeast the entire trip."

"Yes, that's right," said Kalinski. "Do you remember the markers?"

"I remember," Jozef said. "The guards were following these wooden markers the entire time. I didn't know how they knew where they were going at first, but then I saw the markers. They were about six feet high."

We followed no roads on our trek from Surgut to the camp. The snow would have buried roads, had there been any. We'd followed the guards' trucks through the snow for ten days, but I didn't realize they'd been following markers.

"Good," said Kalinski. "Do you remember there was a stretch of about ten miles, where there were no markers? We marched for about ten miles and then the markers appeared again."

"It was about a day after you left the big forest," added one of Kalinski's men.

Jozef frowned and stared into space, trying to remember. He finally shook his head. "No, that I don't recall."

"We can't figure out how they picked up the markers again."

"I remember," said Patryk.

Kalinski turned to Patryk. "How did they pick the trail back up?"

"There was a steep decline," said Patryk. "When the markers stopped, there was a sudden drop to our left the entire time, but unless you ran over to the edge, you couldn't see it well. They must have been following the edge of the decline."

"Are you sure?"

"He's right," said Tomek. "I remember the decline. But I didn't realize the markers had disappeared. But I saw the decline after the forest, that I am sure of."

"So that's it," said Kalinski. He put his hands together. "We look for a steep decline to our right when the markers disappear. We then stay near the edge until we get to the big forest." He pointed to an imaginary map on the table and some of the men actually stared at the splintered wood. "The markers pick up on the other side of the forest. We will have to walk the periphery of the forest until we hit them."

"I think the markers also disappear a few miles before the camp," said Stefan.

It occurred to me that Stefan would have to make the trip on his bad leg. But if he made it up here the first time, I figured he could do it again.

"Well, the least the guards can do is point us in the right direction," said Jozef.

"Is there someone in your barrack who knows the stars—a sailor, maybe?" asked Kalinski. "Such a man would be invaluable in navigating when the sun is down."

"We'll ask around," answered Jozef.

"There's another thing you should know," one of Kalinski's men said.

Kaz leaned close to me. "Another thing we should know?" he repeated in an acid undertone. "They're the ones who didn't know about the decline."

"A guard told me Surgut lies on a large river," said Kalinski's man. "It is the Ob. We didn't see it when we came up because we crossed the river in the train. But if you hit a large river, you are either east or west of the town."

"If we lose the markers, we'll call for a cab," whispered Kaz.

I wasn't sure, but I thought Kalinski heard him.

"So should we leave together?" Jozef asked.

"That's right," said Kalinski. "It's better if we all go together. That's what I would want. The bigger the number, the smaller the chance of a fatal error."

"I just thought of something," Jozef said. "Do you think you could get hold of that newspaper, the one with the decree?"

"I don't know; why?" Kalinski asked.

"When we get to Surgut, we have no train tickets and no money. We can at least show people the decree."

"Yes, yes," said Stefan. "That's a good idea. If someone refuses to let us on a train, we can produce the decree and tell them they are obstructing a direct order of the Supreme Soviet."

"I will try," said Kalinski. "So, we start out together. But you know how these things go. There are bound to be some separations. If some want to go on their own, God go with them."

# Chapter Three

Some of the men had decided not to leave. About fifteen in one barrack were not leaving because they were not Polish citizens. There were also Poles who were too weak to travel, including two or three prisoners in our barrack alone. Mr. Rakowski said he couldn't leave, and refused to discuss his decision with anyone.

I couldn't blame him; I doubted if he would have survived the trip to Surgut. I felt for those remaining in the camp, but there was nothing I could do for them.

"Don't feel sorry for them just yet," Jozef told me. "They may outlive us."

The camp's storehouses must have been full; I hoped that once we left, the camp supervisors would be more generous toward those remaining behind. Some of the men left food for them—not much, but some. I have to admit, I was never one to share my rations. There simply was not enough for me, let alone someone else, too. Some men had shared with those too weak to work, but they were the ones who knew how to get extra rations.

They gave us our deportation papers. Yuriy, the Ukrainian, received his papers without incident. The guards made us line up single file at the main gate. At five a.m., they started releasing us, checking our papers against their lists one by one.

It was still dark, too early to start out. We had to wait for the sun to appear so we could find the markers. I was grateful that the weather was not bad, only minus twenty degrees centigrade, without clouds or wind. We waited just outside the main gate until dawn, and at about nine a.m., three or four hundred men, in a line five abreast, walked away from the camp.

I had planned to take one last look at the camp as we left, but when the moment came, I forgot.  So I only saw the camp once from the outside: the day I entered.

"A move to your right, a move to your left, shall be considered an attempt to escape," someone from the back yelled as we started out, and some of the men laughed.

The mood was very different from what it had been during our arrival.  Men had come up here with chains on, none of them knowing what awaited them.  Now we were in control; we could make our own decisions, and everyone could speak freely.

"At least the guards pointed us off in the right direction," Kaz quipped when we found the markers less than an hour later.  Rags fluttered atop the markers—wooden poles sticking up five or six feet above the knee-deep snow.

Within an hour, a fight broke out between two men in a group traveling about three hundred yards ahead of us.  One chased the other off the trail, and they wrestled in the snow.

"They must be fighting to see who will get on the train first," said one man.  Another called them fools.

I trudged through the snow with a sack of potatoes on my back and a loaf of bread, cut in quarters, inside my coat.  Three dried fish Kaz had given me were in there, too.

The snow was so cold, it squeaked and crunched beneath my canvas boots, but I'd wrapped my feet loosely in the new strips of cloth I'd traded my watch for, to protect them from frostbite.  I'd learned on the trip to the labor camp the year before that the trick to avoiding frostbite was not to wrap the rags too tightly around your feet.  When wrapped loosely, they allowed a cushion of warm air to develop between your foot and the shoe.  If the wrap was too tight, the cushion of air didn't develop and your foot remained as cold as the outside of your shoe.

Tomek had given me rubber insoles he'd made from a blown rubber tire he'd received in barter with a guard.  He'd cut the tire into ten insoles, each with a flap that covered the top of the foot.

I used my old foot rags as insulation inside my gloves, and the third cloth I'd bartered for became a scarf to cover my face;

unlike the others, I wasn't protected with a beard. The inside of my coat was lined by newspaper, a very effective windbreaker.

I also had a knife from Tomek and the flint rock and nail Jozef had given me. Whenever we stopped to rest, I tried to start a fire by striking the nail against the rock, but I'd had no success yet. I tried to hold the rock and grass root at the proper angle in one hand while striking the rock with the nail, but no sparks lit the grass. I watched some of the men adeptly creating fires from nothing more than fine pieces of bark, and wondered if I'd ever master their technique.

We walked across snow-covered fields for about five hours. As the sun set, men fanned out from the main group, watching for the markers so we wouldn't lose our way. As it got darker, one group stayed at the old marker while the other roved forward, looking for the next one in the wan light of a quarter moon. Those who had remained behind followed the other group's voices to the new marker. We crept through the darkness a hundred yards at a time.

The quarter moon set around nine p.m., about six hours after sunset. As I stumbled blindly through the snow, I remembered the truck lights I'd followed when I'd come up to the camp. We could have used those lights now.

Eight more hours into the march, the group started to split up, just as Kalinski had predicted. One group wanted to camp for the night, and our group wanted to continue. Our group, which consisted of our barrack, Kalinski's barrack, and one other, continued to march an hour and a half longer, then we decided to camp, as well.

We settled in a wooded area, where the trees would break the wind. Some of the men drew ax blades from their packs and cut branches from the trees for fires.

I remembered the rules about sleeping in the snow from my trip to the camp. There was no sleeping without a fire. If you fell asleep without a fire, you would not wake up; you entered the sleep of death. No one slept more than two or three hours. Sleep more than a few hours, and you risked the death sleep, even with a fire going. While half the men slept, the other half stayed on guard. After several hours, those that were sleeping were awakened, and it was their turn to watch the others and the fire.

No feet near the fire; I remembered that, too. Feet numbed by hours of marching generated fears of frostbite, and it was tempting to put your frozen feet near the fire. But once the numbness faded, you'd discover the fire had burned your feet. On my trip up, one man burned his feet so badly, he couldn't walk. Take your shoes off and rub your feet hard, the old hands had told me. Then sit cross-legged near the fire, with your feet under your thighs. If your knees could take the heat, so could your feet.

As branches came off the trees, I joined others in stripping bark off the trunks while some men built snow banks about five feet high in an arc around the campsite, with the open end away from the wind. They scooped away some of the snow at the base of the bank to maximize protection from the wind. It was the wind, not the snow that killed. We threw the bark over the snow at the base of the bank for the men to sleep on, and piled some to one side for kindling.

While this was going on, several men gathered around a man who knelt over a tiny mound of grass roots, forming a human windbreak as he tried to coax a spark from a flint rock. They murmured their satisfaction as the fire caught, and built it up right in the opening left in the snowbank. Someone threw a pot full of compacted snow near the fire to melt for drinking water.

Once the fire was going, I removed the rags wrapping my hands under my gloves and used them to cover my feet while I dried my boots and foot rags by the fire. I noticed Stefan rubbing his left knee. He'd had no problems keeping up with the rest of us, but I wondered how badly his leg was bothering him. Sparks flew into the night sky when some of the men tossed their potatoes into the fire to bake. That night, I saved my potatoes and ate only my bread.

There'd been little talking during the march; talking drained you of energy rapidly. But now, I could hear the murmur of quiet conversations as I curled up on the bark to sleep.

We slept in two-hour rotations; after we all had two sleeping periods, we started the second day of our march. No one had died in the night; one hundred and fifty of us trudged under a clear, cloud-free sky. The clear weather held into the night; once the sun set, we traveled by the light of a gibbous moon.

There was about three hours of darkness between the setting of the moon and the rising of the sun. This slowed things down again. Some men tried to use burning brands from the fire as torches, but the wind defeated the flames. With dawn, the pace increased, and we now understood we had to be more productive during the daylight hours. The pace grew to a near run through the snow. Those in front broke fresh powder, dropping back when the task exhausted them and letting others take over, and a natural rotation developed. Some were faster than others, and the line lengthened as the day went on. There was no more laughter; this was harder than anything we remembered from the march up.

The markers followed natural clearings between wooded areas, which alternated with vast open fields. The markers designated a path wide enough to allow a truck to pass, and it was not always the shortest route. But we dared not wander off the path.

We traveled for three more days. The moon was still bright, but now it didn't rise until about four hours after sunset. Some commented from time to time that there were no footprints on the trail at all; the other group must have been lagging.

On day six, we entered a large valley. The day was cloudy and for the first time since we left the camp, a snow flurry developed. If it persisted into the night, the clouds would block the moonlight, making it harder to find the markers and slowing travel. We walked briskly all day and continued at a much slower pace, once the sun set. We camped in the woodless valley and built our snow banks. Some men had been smart enough to carry one or two sticks of wood on their backs from our last rest stop, where there'd been enough wood for several fires, so we had a fire despite the lack of trees.

The next morning, the snow picked up in intensity, making it more difficult to spot the markers, even in daylight. We continued forward at a crawl. The wind picked up, and some men worried that a blizzard approached. Over the next few hours, visibility got progressively worse. Some of the men wanted to stop until the weather improved, but others maintained that we should continue until we found a wooded area. As it started to get dark, the winds started coming in gales.

When I saw that those ahead of me had stopped and gathered to talk, I hurried up to hear what they said.

"We have to camp here," someone yelled. "There is no use in going on."

"If this is a blizzard, it can go for days," Jozef yelled back. "If we wait here, we'll freeze to death."

"Where will we go? We can't see the markers."

"We'll look for wood," said Jozef.

"If we go looking for a forest, we'll lose the markers," a man protested.

"If this is a blizzard, you'll lose the markers in the drifts anyway," said Jozef.

"You don't know this is going to be a blizzard," yelled another man. "It may stop by morning."

"This is going to be a blizzard," yelled yet another. "Every time we have had wind this strong, it was a blizzard."

Someone approached Jozef. I couldn't see him well, but it looked like Kalinski. "If we go and lose sight of the markers, we have no chance," he said. "On our trip up, the trail was never more than a day away from a wooded area. We'll build banks and wait here. When things are better, we'll follow the markers until we come across a forest."

"We can lose the markers anyway when the drifts come," said Jozef.

"If the wind can cover them up, it can just as quickly uncover them," responded Kalinski.

"We'll find wood and make fires," said Jozef. "After the storm, we'll just head southwest. We don't need the markers. We'll go by the sun and the moss."

"The only way to stay warm is to keep moving," yelled Stefan.

A strong gust almost knocked me over. A man next to Kalinski shook his head. "If we head off now and look for a forest, there is no guarantee we will find it. Even if we do, we'll lose the markers."

"If the markers are within twenty-four hours of a forest, why not start now?" asked Stefan.

"You won't know if you're going in the direction of the markers," Tomek replied.

To my own amazement I yelled out, "The markers don't follow the forests, it's just the nature of the terrain."

Kalinski shook his head. "No, no I think we should build camp here. You know what the Siberians say about snow. They don't care about snow; all they worry about is the wind. We'll make big banks and stay close together. We'll keep each other warm until this is over."

"We'll slowly freeze to death," said Stefan. He and Jozef walked a short distance away.

Kaz had joined the group as the men talked. "There's no good choice," he said to me as we walked over to Stefan and Jozef.

Jozef looked very disturbed. He wasn't the type to change plans and go against Kalinski.

"Leaving the markers is risky," said Stefan to Jozef. "What will we do after the storm passes?"

"If we can't find the markers after the storm, we'll go by the sun and the moss," said Jozef. "The town is southwest of here. If we hit the river that guy was talking about, we'll know we're in the area." He sighed. "Look Stefan, I don't know which is the better choice; it all depends on the size of this storm. But sitting here waiting for good weather is the quickest way to die. It happens all the time out here."

Some wanted to stay and others wanted to continue; most didn't know what to do. Kaz and I joined others who watched the men building banks for the camp. None of us helped. I could read the minds of the men around me: were the banks shelters, or graves? I didn't know, and neither did they. But we would freeze to death if we stood around much longer. What was I going to do? Either make a bank, or seek the woods. I stared at the banks in front of me. They looked like white tombstones. Something told me to run.

"Screw Kalinski," said Kaz. "We don't have to listen to him."

"I don't like these banks," I said. "They look scary."

"Screw Kalinski and screw his markers," said Kaz.

"What's Jozef mean about the moss?" I asked.

"What?"

"Jozef said something about using the moss—what did he mean?"

"We are going to look for woods," yelled Jozef to everyone. "Come with us if you want."

Men started to divide, but not according to barrack this time; this was a decision everyone had to make for himself. My decision was made—I was going with Stefan and Jozef. I'd planned to escape with them before, why should I do anything different now? Besides, my father had told me to look for my brother.

Tomek and Yuriy decided to stay with the camp. Kaz joined our group. I didn't see Patryk.

Jozef walked over to Kalinski. I couldn't hear what they were saying, but Kalinski threw his arm out several times, and pointed at the ground. He was obviously yelling at Jozef. The wind blew stronger; it cut right through my clothes. We had to start moving soon. Jozef just stood there with Kalinski. I wondered why Jozef put up with him.

He finally walked away. "Stubborn ass," he muttered as he walked by me.

About fifty of us left. We started out in what we thought was a southerly direction. The wind drove the snow before it; we couldn't see further than our outstretched arms. To prevent separation, we traveled in pairs, holding the coats of the men ahead of us. We walked with our heads completely down to protect our faces from the wind—there was nothing to see anyway. We had no idea where we were headed; we could have been traveling in a circle.

The snow built up on our clothes, on our bent heads, in the beards of the men; we looked like snowmen. After marching for many hours, I started to get worried about my feet. They had stopped hurting and that was a bad sign.

The sky lightened, but the wind and snow continued. This was a full-blown blizzard. The day never really developed; thick clouds obscured the sun, and we marched through perpetual dusk until darkness descended again. I ate while I walked—I needed the energy to march and I saw no reason to save food now.

After marching for about two hours in almost total darkness, someone yelled, "Woods!"

We entered a small copse and immediately began chopping wood, but we could not get a fire started. We had dry grass root and even fine, dry pieces of bark, but the wind was too strong. Six of us surrounded the man with the flint rock, standing as close together as we could, but the wind still managed to gust through.

Finally, one of the men built a snow bank, crawled into it, and lay down with his back to the opening. We waited anxiously outside as he struck the flint rock again and again; finally we heard a muffled exclamation, and he backed out of his snowy cavern with a small, glowing piece of bark. He transferred the tiny flame to a small stack of sticks. It took several hours to get the fire going.

"Feet away, feet away from the fire," some yelled.

As I warmed up, the stiffness left my joints and they started to hurt. I was afraid to look at my feet. I kept them a good distance from the fire, but they slowly started to burn anyway. I knew it was frostbite, and only a matter of time before I knew how bad. A slight case of frostbite could mean only redness and discomfort for a day or two. If it was more severe, blisters formed; I had heard of cases where the feet became gangrenous.

Others started complaining of frostbite too, even one man who had real boots protecting his feet. Some said rubbing your feet with snow relieved frostbite, but I found it hurt even more.

I decided to eat my last fish and sat down by the fire with Kaz as he mended his gloves with needle and string. Someone walked up behind us and asked Kaz to repair his gloves, too. I recognized the voice and turned around to greet Patryk. I hadn't seen him since we'd left the others. I had not known whether or not he joined our party. Patryk joined us by the fire and talk turned to those who'd remained in the valley. We wondered how they were doing.

I sat with the others by the fire and waited for the storm to abate. It lasted another three days. Someone claimed that two men from our group were missing, but nobody dared to go out and look for them. All we could do was sit and watch the snow. At night, we occasionally heard the howling of wolves. "Don't worry," the others told me, "if a pack of wolves came upon one or two men, they might take an interest, but our numbers and the fires will keep the wolves away."

I kept an eye on my feet while we waited. The burning went away, though I still had a few blisters. I eyed the snow around our camp; it was about waist high but there were some drifts that were clearly over my head. I wondered how we'd travel through it.

A relatively strong sun followed the storm and Stefan said the sun should help evaporate the snow. As the sun finally came out, some men noticed a depression that ran along the edge of the forest. They were convinced it must be the edge of a lake.

37

They headed out to the area and cleared the snow, then shouted back at us that it was indeed a lake—a wide, frozen lake.

I didn't realize why the others were so excited until someone started bending a needle into a fishhook. I'd fished with my father and brother many times on our land, but always in the summer months; I'd never considered ice fishing. I went down to the lake and watched them cutting into the ice with knives. As they broke through, water gushed out of the hole, washing several fish onto the surrounding ice. They looked like trout.

"It's the difference in the pressure," a man beside me explained. His name was Zbyszek. He was of medium build and had a brown beard without any gray; I guessed he was about forty. "The water gushes out because of the difference in pressure," he continued. "The fish were attracted to the tapping."

We collected the fish while several men started making lures. They made a large loop right at the end of a length of string, and attached the hook at the end of the loop. They used fish eyes as bait. It occurred to me that I still had my fish heads in my coat. I was saving them for when I was desperately hungry, but now, I realized, I had my own bait.

"The loop makes the lure flutter on the way down—that's what attracts the fish," said Zbyszek. "Without the flutter, the fish won't even notice the bait."

Everyone got into the act, and several more holes were cut through the ice. There was plenty of string, but few needles for hooks. Kaz gave out a few needles to men who promised to give him fish in return. He was unwilling to give me one of his last few needles, as he feared that bending them would make them useless for mending. I decided to fashion a hook, albeit a crude one, from the nail I had been trying to start fires with. I used my fish eyes as bait and I got a bite within the first hour, but I didn't actually catch a fish for several hours.

Our catch was not great but it was large enough that everyone agreed to stay for one more day, even though the weather had improved. The food supplies we'd brought from the labor camp would not last much longer, and we might not find a spot like this again for a long while.

I caught eight fish the next day, and ate three. I caught more than some of the others. My father had taught me how to tease fish a long time ago, but some of the men, like Patryk, were fishing for the first time.

Some of the men skimmed the fat from underneath the skin of the fish they ate and applied it to lips ulcerated by scurvy and wind. Others preserved their catch by smoking the fish, and they taught me how to do this.

The trick in smoking a fish properly, they said, was not to place it too close to the fire, or it would cook. Cooked fish would last only several days, but a properly smoked fish would be preserved for a very long time. They showed me how to place the fish just far enough from the fire so the temperature was just slightly higher than body temperature. The heat evaporated all the water from the fish, drying it completely. The problem was that it took several days to properly smoke the fish, and we were moving out the next day. So we settled for fish that was partially cooked and partially smoked. They told me it would have been a lot better to cure the fish first, but nobody among us had any salt. My fish would be eaten soon enough, anyway.

Jozef and Stefan were making the rounds, and they eventually made their way over to Kaz, Patryk, and me.

"How are you holding out, Andrzej?" asked Stefan.

"I caught a few," I said.

"We searched the area and we can't find the markers," said Jozef. I would have been alarmed, but he said this like it really didn't matter.

"What's the plan?" asked Kaz. "Tell me you have a plan."

Jozef laughed. "We'll head southwest," he said. "We'll navigate using the sun and the moss."

"What does that mean, anyway?" I asked. "What do you mean, 'the moss'?"

"Come on," said Jozef. He walked us up to a tree and said, "If you'll notice, the moss on trees only grows on the protected side. Now, in winter, the moss is sometimes green, but it can be white, as well. On a cloudy day or even during the night, you can see the moss and use it to navigate."

He touched the tree with just the tip of his glove. "Notice how smooth it is compared to the bark. Even if the night is pitch black, you can feel the smooth side where the moss has grown and where the sun shines."

"Well, I'll be damned," said Kaz as he put his hand on the trunk. "You know, I never noticed that. Where do you learn this stuff?"

"The army," answered Jozef. "They teach you to survive."

Both Patryk and Kaz were city fellows and didn't seem to know how to survive on this land any more than I did. Patryk didn't say anything; I knew he wouldn't admit he'd learned something from Jozef.

"What was the name of that river?" asked Kaz. "The one that Surgut lies on."

"The Ob," answered Stefan.

"How will we know it's the Ob when we come across it?" I asked.

"We'll know," said Jozef. "It's supposed to be a large river, fifty to a hundred yards wide. We'll know it when we see it."

"How will we know which way to turn when we reach the river?" asked Patryk.

"We won't," said Stefan.

"Let's worry about reaching the river first," said Jozef. "That is our immediate objective. You always have some settlement near rivers, even in remote areas."

"That's what some of the others have told us," said Stefan. "Even out here, we should eventually come across a home along the river, even if we are a hundred miles from Surgut."

We headed southwest the next morning. The air was cold, but there was little wind and no clouds. We avoided the tall drifts and tried to always keep a forest in sight. Since we didn't have to stop to look for markers, our pace quickened, despite the deep snow. However, as the temperature rose slightly, the snow melted on our pants; we were totally wet from the waist down. We were uncomfortable but worse, the chill dampness caused shivers.

We couldn't keep up our pace for more than five or six hours at a time before stopping to build a fire and rest. After several days in this wilderness, I understood what Jozef meant when he'd told me in the camp that flint rock could mean the difference between life and death. I made it a point to keep bark and small sticks in my pockets. At least wood was drier now, and it was easier to start fires.

The half moon and the sun now rose and set at the same time, but our routine was now independent of both the sun and moon; we followed the moss on the trees. Jozef was right; even in total darkness, I could walk up to a tree, brush off the snow, feel for the moss, and know where south was.

On the next day, when the men on watch woke everyone up to continue the march, Markowski didn't get up.

"He's dead," said a man standing over Markowski.

"It's impossible," said Zbyszek. "There was nothing wrong with him." He ran over to Markowski and tried to wake him up. He opened Markowski's left eyelid with his thumb and index finger, then stood. "I don't get it," he said. "He was fine. He was next to the fire; he did everything right."

"Are you sure he's dead?" Stefan asked as he walked up to us. He knelt and examined Markowski himself, then rose. "Let's cover him up," he said quietly.

We couldn't dig into the frozen ground. The men covered him up with snow, made a cross out of sticks, and placed it on his grave.

The next day, we came to a frozen river almost a hundred yards wide. It had to be the Ob. We were either east or west of Surgut, but nobody knew which direction to go. We decided to camp at the river and fish.

Kaz and I were helping Stefan light a fire when one of five men around a hole cut in the ice yelled up to us, "Hey, the water smells funny."

I didn't pay any attention, but Stefan stared at the man for a long moment, then walked down to the river. Kaz and I followed him.

"The water smells funny," the man repeated when we arrived.

"Like kerosene or something," said another as he held the water to his nose.

We took turns sniffing the cold water and tried to interpret the smell. I thought they were right; it was contaminated with something.

"We're downstream," said Zbyszek. "We must be downstream from Surgut."

"It could be from another town," said Stefan.

"Possible," said Jozef. "But Surgut must be the only town large enough to pollute a river within hundreds of miles."

It wasn't a wild guess now. We decided to camp the night and start upriver in the morning.

# Chapter Four

Less than two days' walk along the river, we started to smell sulfur in the air. Not long after that, we saw houses in the distance.

We entered the town in the late night. Road signs told us we were in Surgut. The town looked very poor; wooden shacks lined the dirt roads. *It's a good thing there's no one on the streets,* I thought as I trudged along with the others. *The sight of fifty bearded men marching together at this hour must look frightening.*

We wandered around, looking for the train station without success until we saw an elderly woman pushing a cart filled with empty milk bottles. She was not startled to see us at all—she seemed to know that we were looking for the train station. When Jozef spoke to her in Russian, she pointed us in the right direction.

Within half an hour, we crossed the train tracks and approached a long wooden building with a towering statue of Stalin out front. Several sleds waited beside the statue. The station seemed very busy, considering the time and location. People stood near the doors and leaned against the wall. As we got closer, I saw that they all wore the same prison issue clothing we wore, and they were bearded as well. I didn't recognize anyone; these people were not from our camp. I felt their eyes on me—on all of us—as we approached the building.

A bearded man of about forty standing near the station's entrance asked us in Polish, "Are you Poles?"

"Yes," said Stefan.

"Is there a train headed out?" asked Jozef.

The man ignored him. "They just let you out?" he asked Stefan.

"Yes, and you?"

"Three weeks ago. What camp are you from?"

"A lumber camp, about three hundred miles northeast," answered Stefan. "Where were you?"

"The coal mines," he said. "But there are women and children here, from another camp. Did they give you deportation papers?"

I didn't like this man. We'd just gone through hell to get here, and he wanted to chitchat.

"Yeah," said Stefan. "How long have you been waiting?"

"Almost two weeks."

"Is a train coming?" Stefan asked.

"They say there should be one here soon."

"Meaning what?"

"Who knows, with these people? A few days, I hope. It's Satan's system." He leaned forward. "Have you heard about the army that's forming?"

"Yeah, we know." Stefan brusquely dismissed that topic. "Where will the train go? Did they tell you? Will it connect with the Trans-Siberian Railway?"

"That's what we're hoping. The train is supposed to take us to Sverdlovsk. The Trans-Siberian Railway goes through Sverdlovsk."

"How much are the tickets?" asked Jozef.

The man shook his head and waved his arm. "Don't worry about that. You don't need a ticket. You can just get on—they told us so. They want to get rid of us. The militia stops by here every day and asks about the train, too. They want us out of here; they don't want us talking to the locals."

Stefan's gaze slid over the man's shoulder. "Is it heated inside?" he asked.

"Not much," the man said, then tried again: "What have you heard about the army?"

"All they told us is that the army is forming in the south," said Jozef. "Do you know any more?"

The man shook his head. "That's what we heard—southern Russia."

I followed Jozef through the entrance, into a dimly lit hall about thirty yards long and fifteen yards wide. A foul smell hung in the air, but it was warm—warm enough for us—probably five to ten degrees centigrade above zero. Sleeping people covered the floor, many of them children.

Stefan and Jozef moved away to gather information from those waiting in the station, but I found a space on the crowded floor and dropped immediately. Like the others, I hadn't slept more than two or three hours at a time for the past few weeks.

I slept almost twenty-four hours; I awoke to late night again. As soon as I'd gathered my senses, I got up and walked through the station in search of my family. *I can't see the faces of those sleeping,* I told myself when I found no one. *They may be here.* I returned to Kaz and Patryk, who had been watching my potatoes for me, and mutely shook my head.

The man in front of the station told the truth—they would let us get on a train to Sverdlovsk without tickets, Kaz reported as I sat down beside him. Those waiting in the station were all Polish deportees from two other camps; one a prisoner camp like ours, located about seventy-five miles to the east, and the other a camp for women and children about fifty miles to the northwest. They'd arrived before the blizzard that had caused the trains' delay. We were the first ones to make it here from our camp.

The camps for the women and children, called posiolki, were very different from ours, Kaz told me. The posiolki had no guards, barbed wire, or dogs; the women and children had nowhere to go if they tried to escape. They were paid for their work, and bought food in small shops in the camp. They'd even been brought from the camp to the station by horses and sleds.

I hoped my mother and little Michal were treated that well. I noticed some teenagers my age with their mothers in the station, and wondered what it would have been like to be in a posiolek with my mother.

We had access to a well, but no food was given out in the station and those who were waiting had been living on their own provisions. The men from the mining camp had lumps of coal in their sacks that they wanted to trade for food. They had no takers from us.

Patryk decided to go to sleep and Kaz and I gnawed on raw potatoes while we watched his things. We wasted nothing now; we even ate the skins. I never thought I would be eating the skins of raw potatoes. As I chewed, the meat of the potato ground against the skins, which tasted like soil no matter how well they were washed. Grimacing, I considered building a fire outside and baking the potatoes, but the locals may not have liked that, and I didn't want to attract the militia.

"May we have some potatoes, sir?" a girl's voice asked, and I jerked my head up. Three girls stood in front of me. They were thin and frail looking. I hadn't even seen them approach. The oldest, about ten years old, had spoken; the other two were much younger, and didn't look at me.

I didn't know what to say. I hated eating raw potatoes, but they were my potatoes. I only had about twenty, though I still had some smoked fish.

"Sure," Stefan said from behind me. He walked up and handed each of them a potato. "What is your name?" he asked the oldest.

She bit into the potato and didn't answer until she'd swallowed the morsel. "Jola. Are you going to find the army?"

"Is your mother with you?" asked Stefan.

"Mom's dead," said one of the younger girls. She scraped at the potato with her upper teeth.

"These are your sisters?" Stefan asked Jola.

She nodded and took another bite.

"Who is taking care of you?"

"I am," Jola replied. "I'm almost twelve."

"Do you have any other relatives here?" asked Stefan.

"There is Mrs. Wertowski, but she doesn't like me," said Jola.

"Is she a relative?" Stefan asked.

"No."

"Are you waiting for the train?" asked Kaz. Jola nodded. "We are going to find the army."

"The army?" I asked. "Why?"

"The army will take us home," she answered.

"Where are you from?" asked Stefan.

"Przemysl."

"You don't have any food?" I asked.

"We had potatoes and some bread, but we ate it all," she said. "Some of the men give us food."

I didn't know why she thought I should give her my potatoes. I'd had to trade my watch for them. But I was glad Stefan had given them food.

Kaz poked the little girls in the stomach, but they didn't laugh. There was no joy in their faces. *They're the same age as Michal,* I thought, watching the younger ones hold their potatoes with both hands as they thanked us and walked away.

"I bet the women sent them over here for food," said Kaz. "They knew we wouldn't turn them down."

Stefan laughed. "You're probably right."

As the sun rose, the light in the station improved and I looked again for my family, without luck. As I wandered, I noticed others studying the far wall of the station. I walked over and saw a large train map of Russia. A thick red line running from Moscow to China marked the Trans-Siberian Railway. The line connected a number of cities I'd never heard of: Irkutsk, Novosibirsk, Omsk, and there was Sverdlovsk, where we were headed. I guessed it lay about seven hundred miles southwest of Surgut.

Kaz and Patryk had been talking to the men from the other camp, who knew more than the man we'd spoken to outside. A Polish army was forming somewhere east of the Volga River. From Sverdlovsk, the Volga River was about five hundred miles directly west. The army could be anywhere in the five hundred miles south of the Volga.

Stefan walked up to me and said, "Andrzej, there's a guy who says he knows where the NKVD sent the officers. Your father is an officer, right?"

"Yes, he's a colonel, but he's retired," I said.

"Go talk to him. He seems credible. He's over there," he said, pointing. "The one with the bad cough."

I joined Jozef, who was talking to a man in his late forties, older than most of us. He had a bad cough, indeed. He could barely finish a sentence without suffering a coughing spasm.

"Excuse me," I said. "I heard you know where the Soviets took the Polish officers. Is this true?"

The man shook his head slowly, as if he didn't know what I was talking about.

"He's one of us," Jozef told the man. "His father is an officer."

"Oh, I see," the man said. "Yes, yes, they put all the officers in one camp, in Kozielsk."

"Where's that?"

"Kozielsk? It's on the other side of the Urals—south of Moscow."

"How do you know they took the officers there?" I asked."

He tried to answer but entered a prolonged spasm of coughing. "I know because I was there," he finally replied. "It was in '39; the camp was filled with officers from all over Poland. We didn't know why they'd put us with the officers, but it didn't matter. We weren't there long. They sent us off after a few days."

"That is exactly when my father was arrested—'39. My father's name is Bartkowski. Did you run across him?" I asked.

"The officers were separated from us. They didn't let us talk to the officers. But there were hundreds of officers. I am sure of that."

"Do you know if they've let them go yet?" I asked.

"Oh, I wouldn't know about that. I've been in this area ever since."

"Thank you," I said, and eagerly returned to study the wall map. This was the best news I'd heard since they told us we could leave the camp.

Kozielsk was not on the map, but Moscow was. Kozielsk had to be quite a way west of the Ural Mountains, and much closer to where the army was forming than Surgut. The decree to release the Polish prisoners must have come out of Moscow. My father's camp must have gotten the word right away, three months earlier, in August. He must be with the new army already.

Fatigue suddenly overcame me. Even though I had only been awake for a few hours, I had to sleep again. When I returned to our area, Patryk was awake. I asked him to watch over my things and promptly fell asleep.

I woke when Kaz pulled me up by my shoulders, yelling, "Wake up, wake up!"

I jumped up; I had no idea how long I'd slept.

Kaz had his sack on his shoulder. "A locomotive is here," he said. "A locomotive is pulling into the station."

I could hear the engine. It was barely light outside. "Is it dawn or dusk?" I asked.

"Get your things," he said.

"When did it get here?"

"Now—right now! Get your things."

"I didn't know," I said as I picked up my sack. "It's not my fault. I didn't know it was coming and I fell asleep."

"What are you talking about?" he asked. "Just get your things."

We followed others out the door and joined the crowd gathered beside the tracks. The steam locomotive slowly passed by, blowing large clouds of steam into the air. It turned onto a side track and turned off its engine. I saw cattle cars being attached to the steam engine. Word went around that, within an hour, the locomotive would in fact pull a train to Sverdlovsk.

When they opened the car doors, I watched the people entering the cars. I saw no one else from our camp. Not only had the group that camped out in the valley during the blizzard not reached the station; there was no sign of the other group, the one we'd separated from the first night.

The interior of the cattle car I entered was a little different from the cars I'd ridden in on my trip to Siberia. This one had a small stove in the middle with a pipe venting to the outside. I checked the stove; it was cold and empty of fuel. Unlike conditions on the trip up, the car was not overcrowded. I could sit down, even lie down if I wanted to. No one complained about the cattle car or the cold. We were leaving Siberia—that was the important thing.

Jola and her two sisters attached themselves to our group, and me in particular. They followed us into our car and sat down right next to me. Kaz leaned over and whispered that the other women didn't look after them because they hadn't liked the girls' mother. I wished the girls would sit next to Stefan; he had twice as much food as I did.

At daybreak, the train finally left the station and once again I heard that familiar clunking of the wheels against the tracks. We sat with our backs to the walls of the cattle car and waited for Sverdlovsk.

Stefan turned to Kaz and said, "Ask one of the miners to donate some coal."

"Ask them yourself," said Kaz, then added, "How long is this ride going to be?"

"Based on this speed, I would say about thirty hours," said Patryk.

"You're assuming the train won't stop," said Jozef, seated in the back corner. "These trains always stop."

"I meant thirty hours of movement," Patryk quickly added.

"You would think they would throw just a small chunk of coal in there," said Stefan.

"Where exactly is the Volga River?" asked Kaz. "How many miles? Anyone know?"

"Over a thousand," said Jozef.

"It depends on the latitude," said Patryk. "The Volga runs east as you go south."

"East? No way," said Jozef. "The Volga flows southwest into the Caspian Sea."

"That's when you're south of Gorky," said Patryk. "When you're north, the river turns eastward as you go south."

"No way," repeated Jozef. He got up and pointed at the wall of the car as though it was a map. He dragged his finger down the wall, saying, "Here, this is how it flows."

"No, no, no," said Patryk. He got up and drew a curve with his finger that was different from Jozef's.

"So the army is forming east of the Volga?" asked Kaz. "Let's hope we can find the Volga—"

"And hope this army's better than the last," Patryk interjected.

"You mean the army '39?" asked Jozef. "It wasn't the army's fault."

"You guys got slaughtered."

Stefan shook his head, his eyes on the two men. "Oh no," he said. "Here they go again."

"The army had no chance in '39," said Jozef. "It was a political failure."

"Politicians don't fight battles," Patryk argued.

"They wouldn't even let us protect the borders," said Jozef. "Beck was pro-German, and that was fatal."

"Beck, pro-German? No, no, I don't see that," said Patryk. "Beck strongly warned the Germans that an attempt to take Gdansk would lead to war."

"Who is Beck?" I asked Stefan.

"The Polish Foreign Minister before the war," he replied.

"That was in '38," said Jozef. "The Germans backed off after that, like it didn't matter. They should have seen it coming. They didn't want Gdansk, they wanted the whole pie."

"If you're going to blame someone, blame Smigly-Rydz," said Patryk.

"Smigly-Rydz?" asked Jozef. "You have to be kidding."

"Who started them off this time?" asked Stefan. "Was it you, Andrzej?"

"Me? I don't even know what they're talking about."

Jola came up to me and asked, "What are they arguing about?"

"I don't know," I said.

"Can I have a potato?"

"I guess." I gave her one and added two more for her sisters. *But that's it,* I thought. I'd have to get them to ask the others for food.

"How come you keep giving us the smaller ones?" asked Jola.

"What do you mean?" I asked.

"You have bigger potatoes in your sack, I saw them."

"When did you see them?" I asked.

"She went through your things when you were sleeping," said Kaz. "I saw her."

I glared at her. "Don't go through my things."

Stefan had tired of that day's sparring match between Jozef and Patryk. He turned to me and said, "You know, I remember on my trip to Siberia, I saw the most incredible thing. We were all packed in tight, and there was this priest in the car—"

"They arrested priests?" I interrupted.

"Oh, yeah, all the time," he said. "We didn't have a priest in our camp, but there were priests in the other camp I was in. It's something, to see a priest with a long beard. There were times I thought this priest on the train was dead. His eyes were almost always closed and it looked as if he was not supporting his body. Many slept standing up, but when the doors opened, the others would quickly awaken and get out of the car. But we had to drag this priest out, and it took a while to wake him from his stupor. Once or twice, the guards even thought he was dead."

"That's a disease," said Kaz. "I heard of that; it's called cataplexy."

Stefan nodded, but didn't look as though he'd really heard what Kaz said. "Later, in the camp, I told him how I thought he'd died on the train. And he told me the most extraordinary thing. He said he had been praying the entire time. He was repeating Gregorian chants to himself over and over, day after day."

"Why were they arresting priests?" I asked.

"They arrested anyone they thought we considered a valuable member of society," answered Jozef. "In each Polish town, they picked out those they thought would object to their new system—anyone who had any form of authority whatsoever: mayors, lawyers, policemen, bankers, priests, doctors, you name it. Satan's system. Their plan was to transform a democratic society into an amorphous mass that they could then mold to their liking."

I suddenly remembered what I'd seen in the station. "I noticed there were teenagers my age in the station, and they were with their mothers," I said. "Why did they send me to an adult prisoner camp?"

"They didn't like your bloodline," said Jozef. "When they arrested you, they knew your father was an officer in the army. They were worried you would be trouble. They probably thought that, if they sent you to one of the posiolki, you would eventually escape. So they sent you to a place with guards, watchtowers, and barbed wire."

"They sent you there to die, Andrzej," said Stefan. "Whether you died at the age of sixteen or sixty, they sent you to the camp to die."

"They weren't counting on the Germans to invade," said Jozef. "Now, everything is different."

I stared at the orange light coming in through the cracks in the walls of the car. The sun had started to set, and the flashes of light were getting dimmer and dimmer. It never occurred to me that I was being punished because of my father. *But he did nothing wrong!* I thought.

I remembered what my father said the day the war broke out, in September of 1939. He took Stan and I aside; he spoke mainly to Stan, who was nineteen. He told Stan that someone would eventually enlist him into an army, like they had with him in the Great War. He told Stan never to carry anything of value when he was a soldier.

"If your unit takes a town and the men start to pilfer the goods, have nothing to do with it," he said. "If someone hands you a gold ring, throw it in the garbage. When they pay you, exchange it immediately for cigarettes and food you can carry. Hold nothing of any market value whatsoever." In the Great War, he had witnessed many men dying from greed. Greed made them take chances they otherwise would not have taken, he said.

A few weeks after he spoke to us, the NKVD came to our door and began asking questions very innocently. Within the hour, however, they took him away.

# Chapter Five

I woke up when one of Jola's little sisters started to cry intensely.

"It's hunger pains," Jola told us.

Several men offered the girls potatoes and dried fish.

*We must be close to Sverdlosk,* I thought. We had been on the train for almost a week. On the second day out of Surgut, the train had stopped in the middle of nowhere for about a day and a half, just as we expected, and a second time after that, but we had traveled nonstop since then. As I had hoped, some of the miners finally burned small pieces of coal in the stove. The air was still cold, but the stove helped somewhat.

Several hours after midnight, about an hour after I awoke, the train finally arrived in Sverdlovsk.

Some of the men groaned as we entered a station much larger than the one in Surgut. Over a thousand people waited inside the station; they all appeared to be Polish deportees converging from the camps. Some approached us for money and food, but we told them we had nothing.

Everywhere I looked, I saw people sleeping. I learned later that many of them were sick from dysentery and typhoid fever. We were warned not to drink the water at the station. "Better to go out for a walk and collect some clean snow," they told us. Many severely malnourished deportees had reached the station on their last legs and then died right there in the station. Their bodies were stacked in the snow outside.

We learned that a westbound train on the Trans-Siberian Railway would arrive in a few days, but unlike Surgut, they would not let people get on this train without tickets. The tickets cost fifty rubles per person.

I was surprised to see some of the men and women we'd traveled with from Surgut, including men from our camp, pull out money they'd had hidden to buy tickets. Kaz and I looked at one another. We had no money. Would we join others in the station with no money, who waited for a miracle?

"Does anyone have any rubles whatsoever?" Jozef asked the ten of us who'd stayed together since leaving the camp.

"I still have a watch," Patryk offered.

"We'll have to sneak on the westbound train when it arrives in a few days," said Jozef. "Before then, we'll have to go out to the tracks and see how the whole thing operates. If an eastbound train comes, we can study the routine, how they let passengers aboard."

Zbyszek, the ice fisherman, approached. "What a mess," he said. "Do you have any money?"

"No," Jozef replied.

"I just heard that some people go to local farms and work for rubles. Some have made enough to leave," Zbyszek said.

"We're four months late already," said Jozef. "Let's see how easy it would be to sneak on a train."

"And if they catch you?" asked Zbyszek.

Don't forget about them," added Stefan, pointing at Jola and her sisters, who continued to follow us everywhere.

"I know," answered Jozef. "Let's split up and look around. Maybe someone is organizing an orphanage. Stefan and I will check the schedules and go observe the tracks. Someone has to find out if they're handing food out, at least for the kids."

"I'll go," said Kaz.

Jozef nodded. "Someone has to stay and watch our things. Andrzej, why don't you go ask around about the orphanage?"

I liked the idea. Not only could I unload these kids, but I could look for my family, as well.

We left Patryk watching our things and split up. I took the girls with me. We walked between crying children and semi-comatose adults. The closest I came to finding anyone who might be associated with an orphanage was a woman with six small children gathered about her. A handkerchief framed her tired face.

"Excuse me," I said as I approached her. "I have some orphans in need of a guardian. Are these your children?"

"These aren't orphans," she said abruptly. "They are mine and my sister's."

I wasn't sure if she was just surprised or insulted. "Do you know if anyone is taking care of orphans?"

"There are more and more orphans each day," said the woman. "We give them some food, but there is not even enough for my own."

"No, I mean, is there a guardian from some relief organization? Is anyone gathering the orphans together?"

"There's nothing like that here," she said, then added, "my sister is out trying to find enough money for the tickets. Would you have some rubles to spare—I mean, for my children? I have to get them to the army."

I was standing there with three orphans and she wanted money from me. "No, I'm broke," I said. "I'm just trying to help these children." I turned to point to the girls, and saw they were talking to some other children.

"I can't help you," the woman said as she rose and walked towards one of her children.

As we moved further down the station, I overheard someone in a group of men say, "Kozielsk." I got closer and listened in.

"Kozielsk," one of them repeated. "If your brother is an officer, they took him to Kozielsk."

I now had further confirmation of where my father might have been.

A man with a real fur hat interjected with, "You know, not all the officers went to Kozielsk. Some of them were taken to another camp in Starobielsk."

"Where is Starobielsk?" I blurted. When they stared, I told them about my camp and my father.

"Near the Black Sea," one of them said. "Just north of the Black Sea."

"South of Moscow," added the man in the fur hat. "From what I heard, most went to Kozielsk, but some officers were taken to Starobielsk."

"Thank you," I said, and walked away, my mind sifting through possibilities. Even if they'd taken my father to Starobielsk, it was south of Moscow, still way west of the Ural Mountains and even closer to where the new army was forming. He still would have heard about it before I did. He could be waiting there for me.

As I walked back to the place where Patryk watched over our belongings, I couldn't keep from grinning. I might see my family soon! But the smile vanished when I saw that four other small children had joined Jola and her sisters. "Who are these kids?" I asked Jola.

"They're hungry," she said.

"Where are their parents?"

"They don't have any," she said.

"Why are they following us?"

"For some potatoes."

*Great,* I thought, then asked, "Why did you tell them we have food?"

"They're hungry," Jola repeated.

A woman approached me and asked for rubles. "I'm sorry," I told her gruffly, and just kept walking.

Jozef and Stefan had also returned. They'd heard the same thing I had—there was no relief organization here. Some people had gone to the post office and sent telegrams to the Polish embassy in Moscow asking for help, but the telegrams were never answered. Jozef said it was because the new Polish government running the embassy was filled with Soviet puppets.

Kaz returned and reported that he hadn't found food, but he did hear that every Polish deportee was supposed to receive fifty rubles and a train ticket to the destination of his or her choice as they left the camp, according to the decree. Some camps were doing just that, making it much easier for the deportees to travel. We, of course, had received nothing.

Jozef looked at Patryk and hesitated but finally asked, "Patryk, does your watch work?"

"Yes," Patryk replied.

"Would you be willing to swap it to allow us to get on a train?"

"Well, we've got to get out of here," said Patryk.

"Can I borrow it to see if we can get a worker to sneak us on a train?" Jozef asked. "You can come along."

"Go ahead, take it." Patryk handed the watch to Jozef. "We have to get out of here."

"Want to come along?" asked Jozef.

"No, no, just take it and bring it back; I'll watch the things," said Patryk.

"You'll get it right back," said Jozef. He looked at the children, then at me. "Who are these kids?"

I just shrugged helplessly.

Jola approached Jozef. "They have no mothers," she said. "They're hungry."

Jozef turned to me. "You were supposed to find a guardian for these kids and you come back with four more?"

The others laughed. I raised my arms. "I don't know who they are," I protested. "They just kept following me."

Jozef waved my protest away and turned back to the newcomers: three boys and a girl aged between six and ten. With Jozef's prompting, they revealed that two of the boys were brothers and the other two were from separate families. They all had the same story—their mothers had died at the station. One of the boys even pointed to the bench where his mother died. We gave them each a potato and, as they chomped on their raw potatoes, Kaz went out with a tin can to get snow for drinking water. Stefan and Jozef went off again. Left with the children, I sat down, shaking my head.

\*\*\*

The day passed into night and still Stefan and Jozef had not returned. I heard a train come and go and hoped they got a good look at how passengers were put aboard. Patryk was worried that Stefan and Jozef had bought two train tickets with his watch, and were gone.

"They're not the type," Kaz said, and I nodded, trying to reassure Patryk.

"I know," Patryk admitted, "but these are desperate times, and men will do desperate things."

Stefan and Jozef finally returned and gave Patryk back his watch.

"Give us your sacks—we need empty sacks," Stefan said, "and two men to come with us."

"Why?" I asked, but he said they would explain later. They went off again with Zbyszek and another man.

We sat against the wall amidst the sleeping children, and waited.

"What do you think is going on?" Kaz asked.

"They must have found food," said Patryk.

"I hope so," I said. "I'm running really low." I checked my sack. I was down to seven potatoes, and my fish were all gone.

"Why do all these women want to find the army?" I asked.

"Must be for food and protection," answered Kaz. "Where there is an army, there is food. And who will protect these Polish women in this godforsaken land but a Polish army? It's the only way out of this hellhole."

"I haven't seen anyone we left behind on the trip from the camp to Surgut," I said. "Have you?"

Patryk shook his head.

"No," Kaz said. "I was wondering about the same thing." He turned to Patryk and asked, "Do you have any brothers or sisters?"

"A brother," Patryk replied.

"How old?" I asked. I didn't ask Patryk questions often. Not because he looked down on me or ignored me, but because he gave me a strange feeling, like he wasn't really there.

"Sixteen, now," said Patryk.

"Did they let him stay with your mother?" I asked.

"I think so. They separated me from them, but I hope they kept my brother and mother together."

"Why did they send you to a prisoner camp?" I asked. "They could have sent you to one of those posiolki."

"Don't know," said Patryk.

"What were you studying in Lwow, law?" asked Kaz.

Patryk nodded. "I was in my third year."

"They took your father first, in the fall?" I asked.

"Yes, the fall of '39. We heard they were coming back for the families, so we hid at a relative's house. They found us anyway."

"Did they take your relatives, too?" asked Kaz.

"That's who they were coming for," he said with a wry chuckle. "They found us by accident."

We sat in silence for a while. Then I leaned forward, encouraged by his candor, to ask Patryk if he wanted to join the army. But I saw he had fallen asleep.

After about an hour, Stefan and Jozef and the other two men returned with hands in pockets. They sat down in front of us, forming a circle. Patryk woke up.

"We got some," said Stefan, grinning. He pulled his hand out of his pocket and opened it to reveal what looked like grain.

"Easy, easy, don't show it around," murmured Jozef, and Stefan stuck his hand back in his pocket.

"What is it?" asked Kaz, plucking a few of the grains that still clung to Stefan's hand.

"Looks like oat grain," said Stefan. "But I'm not sure."

"It's oat grain," said Zbyszek. "But it's not milled."

"Where did you get it?" I asked.

"Way on the other side of the tracks," said Stefan. "There's a car full of sacks of grain. The door was locked, but we got it open."

I looked closer at the four men, noticing the bulges in their clothing for the first time. Their pockets were full of grain, and

Zbyszek briefly opened the front of his coat to show us the sacks of oat grain underneath.

Kaz frowned at the grain. "How do you eat this?"

"I think you can just crack the kernel with your teeth," said Stefan. He put a grain into his mouth and tried, then grimaced.

"You can soften it with water, but you'll have to crack the kernels first," said Zbyszek.

"You can probably grind it with two stones or, better yet, a stone against concrete," Stefan said. "Won't help me much unless it really softens, not with my teeth."

"Don't show it around," Jozef said again to everyone. "Be subtle with it. Once they see someone broke into a car, they'll be snooping around."

"I haven't seen any militia here," I said.

"The NKVD is everywhere, Andrzej. Believe me." He turned to Patryk. "I think we may have a way to get on the train. There's a railroad worker who said he would help us, for the right price. I showed him your watch, and he liked it. He said as long as they load the passengers in the dark and there is room in the cars, he will let up to ten of us on, for the watch. He said he couldn't help us if they load the train during the daylight hours; it would be too risky for him. That okay with you?"

"We have no choice," said Patryk.

"There are more than ten of us now, with these kids here," I said.

"Let's hope he can't count," answered Jozef.

Kaz and I found several stones outside the station and cracked some grain on the concrete. We half-filled two tin cans with grain and then filled the rest of each can with compacted snow, so it looked like we were bringing in snow for drinking water. When the snow melted, I tried the concoction, but the grain was still hard. Others told us to give it some time to soften. I found more tin cans and repeated the process, until I had twelve cans lined up against the wall. When I was done, I tried the oatmeal again. It was softer—still gritty, but edible. We gave it to the children, but only Jola would eat it. The others said they wanted potatoes. I figured I could eat the oats and handed out some of my potatoes.

Daylight came and passed. A westbound train arrived and the word went out that it was the Trans-Siberian. As people filed out the door to the platform to show their tickets to the workers, we followed Stefan and Jozef in the opposite direction, out the station's main entrance.

"Walk slowly, not to attract suspicion," Jozef said.

We walked along the eastbound track for about half a mile, then crossed the tracks and headed back toward the station, approaching the train from the rear. The back third of the train did not reach the platform. We hid behind the train here.

Jozef asked Patryk for his watch and went looking for the railroad worker. He returned a few minutes later and signaled us to follow. We ran along the train to one of the last cars, where a worker held the door open. He looked furtively left, then right, and signaled us to get into the car.

"I said ten maximum," he said to Jozef as we clambered in.

"That's what we have—ten," answered Jozef.

The man had no time to count us. We all got in within seconds. Jozef handed him the watch and the man closed the door.

Space in the cattle car was fairly cramped, but it was still not as packed as those on the trip to Siberia. No one complained.

"Maybe we should move away from the door," I said, "in case they open it up to check tickets." If those closest to the door had tickets, I thought, the railway workers might be satisfied and move on.

We moved away from the door, but no one opened it again. After about an hour, the train started to move. We were finally off.

# Chapter Six

I was starting to think it was normal for Jola to sit near me wherever we were. During the train ride, Jola told me about her family.

Her younger sisters were named Marysia and Zosia, she said. They looked our way when they heard their names mentioned, and I saw that they all had the same blue eyes.

"Our mother died when we were living in the camp," Jola explained. The women had to cross a frozen river on their way to work in the forest where the trees were being cut. One morning in late October, the river must not have been completely frozen—her mother fell in. Although someone quickly pulled her out, her clothes were soaked, and she went to work shivering. She could not go back to the barracks because they would not have paid her a full day's work, and the children would not get enough food. A few days later, she developed pneumonia and died within the week. Jola said some of the men buried her in a field where many of the Poles were buried.

"They made a cross for her grave," she said. Her face was expressionless, but her voice sounded dreamy, as though she were distancing herself from the pain. Her voice fell. "Bad things happened on the way to the camp, too."

I didn't think I wanted to hear her next story. Her words reminded me of my mother and Michal, and what they probably went through.

"When the guards were taking us to the camp in Siberia," Jola continued, "the sled we were on hit a bump, and a small child fell off—a boy named Marian. He was only one year old."

The mother screamed and yelled for the guards to stop. But they were not interested in her screams, even when they saw the small boy struggling in the snow.

"They refused to stop," Jola reported.

I imagined the woman's dilemma, how she had to decide within seconds what to do. Should she stay with the rest of her children on the sled, or should she jump off the sled to rescue her youngest child and watch the sled disappear into the snow in the middle of nowhere? If she jumped, the rest of her children would be defenseless, and she would never be reunited with them. If she stayed on the sled, her youngest would die.

"What did she do?" I asked Jola.

She looked away. "I don't remember," she said.

"How can you not remember something like that?" I demanded. "What did she do?"

Jola stared into the air for a while and finally said, "A man made the sign of the cross."

"What?"

"For my mother, when they buried her. A man made the sign of the cross with his hand when they buried my mom, just like back home, like in church." Jola seemed to be in a haze.

It suddenly occurred to me: how could she know the name of a one-year-old if the boy was a stranger? "Was the woman on the sled your mother?" I heard myself ask.

Jola didn't answer, but I could tell I'd guessed correctly. It seemed the woman had decided to stay on the sled.

Jola didn't know where her father was; they took him away when the family was still in Poland. I told her that they were letting all the Poles out of Siberia, including her father, perhaps. I told her not to lose the hope of finding her father. "Keep an eye out when you see people," I said. "You may just find him." The idea excited her; it seemed she presumed a long time ago that he was dead.

The two little brothers who had joined us in the station didn't talk at all, at least not to the adults. The other two children, the ones without siblings, were named Mikolaj and Helena. I feared that Mikolaj was becoming ill. He started complaining of stomach pains and he used the toilet, which was only a hole in the floor of the car, all the time. He continued to eat, however, so we thought that whatever was bothering him may pass.

We were out of potatoes but we still had the oats, thank God. I cracked the kernels and softened the oats with water into cold, gritty oatmeal. I went out for water when the train stopped, being careful not to go too far or the train might leave without me. It happened to many people. We had heard stories of women who were left behind when they went seeking food for their children. We didn't let the orphans out at all. When the train stopped, they removed the bodies of people who'd died in the cars and threw them into the snow. We didn't want the children to see it.

On the fifth day, little Mikolaj spiked a fever. We were worried that he may have dysentery or typhoid fever. Since we had been eating from the same tin cans, we feared we all might be infected. And it would be my fault, too. I was the one Jola and her sisters kept following, and I let the other children tag along with me.

When the train stopped, we asked if there was a doctor in the other cars, but there was no doctor aboard. We could only wait and see what happened. Jozef discovered that our destination was a town called Sarapul, on the Kama River. If Mikolaj didn't get better, we would have to take him to a hospital in Sarapul.

On the sixth day, I learned it was Christmas. Some in the car sang Christmas carols, but I didn't join in. *This is not Christmas, without my family,* I thought.

Mikolaj was still sick when the train finally pulled into Sarapul on the eighth day. He still had a fever and he'd stopped eating. He'd even grown too weak to cry. I carried him into the station, then waited with the others while Jozef went seeking information.

He came back with bad news: Sarapul did not connect with trains headed south. Everyone had to walk one hundred miles south, to a town called Chistopol, for the connection. Mikolaj wouldn't make it.

Stefan and I agreed to take Mikolaj to a hospital while the others waited at the station. We didn't want to leave the poor kid in Russia, but there was nothing else we could do. As we walked through the town, I noticed it was much warmer here.

There was still snow on the ground, but the roads were cleared and it was only a few degrees below freezing.

We took turns carrying Mikolaj until we found the hospital, a long wooden building not much better than the infirmary back at the camp. As we entered, I noticed some of the wood on the benches inside was rotted and split. A porter guarded the entrance. I could tell he was drunk; I did not have to speak Russian to tell he slurred his words. He had a long bushy mustache and wore a drab brown jacket.

"Poles! Poles! And now more Poles!" he yelled. He told us to wait and ambled down the hall.

"We have a sick child!" Stefan yelled after him. The porter waved his hand and said he knew.

A blonde woman in her mid-thirties finally appeared. "You have a sick child?" she asked in fluent Polish. Unfazed by Stefan's beard and our rags, she immediately focused her attention on little Mikolaj. "How long has he been ill?" she asked Stefan.

"He became sick on the train," Stefan said. "He's had a fever for three days."

"Has he had diarrhea?"

"Yes."

"Bloody diarrhea?"

"Yes."

"Is this your child?"

"No, he's an orphan. They told us his mother died in the train station in Sverdlovsk."

She instructed us to bring him into an examining room and then asked us to wait outside. After a few minutes, two women in white rolled him out of the room on a stretcher and the woman approached us.

"He'll have to stay here," she said. "I think he may have typhoid fever."

"Are you a nurse?" asked Stefan.

"No, I'm not a nurse or a doctor," she said. "My name is Irena Rakowska. I work for an orphanage in Buzuluk. There are many Polish orphans like this boy, scattered throughout the area. We usually find them in the train stations. We nurse them until they are fit for travel and then we take them to the orphanage in Buzuluk. I have fourteen other sick children here right now. As soon as they are better, they will go to Buzuluk."

"You are Polish, then?" asked Stefan.

"Yes."

"We've been released from a camp in Siberia," said Stefan.

"I know," she said.

"We're traveling south and we have more orphans with us. We have no money or train tickets, not even for ourselves. We have to get them to an orphanage. Is your orphanage the nearest one?"

"For Polish children, yes," she said.

"Where is Buzuluk?"

"That's where Anders' Army is," she said.

"You mean the Polish Army?"

"Yes, their headquarters is in Buzuluk."

"And where exactly is Buzuluk?"

"It's south of here, in the Orenburg province. You have to get to Chistopol first; from there you can take the trains. How many more orphans do you have?"

"Six."

"Six?" She paused, thinking. "I guess I can arrange it. Are any of the other children sick?"

"No," Stefan replied.

"Arrange what?" I asked.

"A truck—a truck to Chistopol."

Stefan's eyebrows rose. "You can arrange a truck to Chistopol? How can you get a truck?"

"We are under the protection of the Delegatura, an organization formed by the new Polish Embassy. They receive the cooperation of the Soviet government and provide us with trucks when we need them. They set up our ward in this hospital."

"Are you with the army, then?" I asked.

"In a sense," she replied. "The orphanages were founded by the army. Can you get the children here?"

"We can, but you see, there are ten of us. Could we get on the truck, too?"

"Since you were kind enough to bring this boy here, I don't see why not. The truck can hold fifty children; you should all fit."

"We will bring them here right now," Stefan said eagerly. He turned to leave, but turned right back. "Who is Anders?" he asked.

"General Anders," she said. "He's the leader."

\*\*\*

We went back to the train station and found the others. We told them we knew the whereabouts of the Polish Army. We told them about Irena Rakowska, the orphanage, and the truck to Chistopol.

Kaz looked up to the sky with his arms outstretched, as if to thank God. "Finally, you remembered about me," he said.

They had news, too. Russian workers at the station said thousands of Polish men had marched through this area about two months ago, headed toward Chistopol. The army.

As we walked back to the hospital, Stefan remembered Jozef was a soldier and ran up to him. "Who is Anders?" he asked. "The woman said the new army is lead by General Anders—she even called it Anders' Army."

"Wladyslaw Anders?" repeated Jozef. "This is very good news. Wladyslaw Anders is a good man, a general; Marshal Pilsudksi appointed him to the rank of general about five years ago."

"He's Polish?"

"Is he Polish? Yeah, he's Polish—as Polish as they come. He's from the Warsaw area," said Jozef. "He was in the Tsar's army in the Great War; I can't believe the Communists agreed to let him lead."

"Maybe they had no choice," said Stefan.

"Maybe. He's a good man," Jozef repeated. "We'll be in good hands. Men would climb a mountain for Anders. He won't let the Soviets use us as cannon fodder, I can tell you that."

We returned to the hospital and approached the drunken porter. "More Poles!" he yelled and told us to wait.

When Mrs. Rakowska came, she told us she must examine the children to make sure they were fit to travel. We waited patiently as she examined each child. When she finished, she disappeared and returned with a large Russian woman carrying a big pot of rice and a stack of bowls. She handed bowls to everyone.

Mrs. Rakowska stood in the middle of the hall and said, "I would like to thank all of you. The children all tell me you have treated them well. They are tired and malnourished but they are not acutely ill. After they eat and rest, I think they will be fit for travel."

She sat down and continued. "I need you to take them to the orphanage. And, if you would be so kind, I have two more children that have recovered and are ready for the trip. I will get a truck for you. I know you don't have money or train tickets; that shouldn't be a problem. I'll try and get a permit for all of you to travel by train from Chistopol to Buzuluk. The Delegatura have given me such permits in the past. Do you all have your deportation papers?"

"Yes," someone said.

"Good," she said. "I will need them for the permit."

"How long before everything is ready?" asked Stefan.

"Let the children rest until at least tomorrow. By then, I should have a truck and your permit. I will take the children for the night. There is a storage room; you may all stay in there for the night."

The children ate their rice and left with Mrs. Rakowska. We asked for more rice, but the woman from the kitchen told us it would cut into tomorrow's rations for the children. She did let us mill our oats, however. We cooked some real oatmeal and went to sleep in a warm room.

The next morning, the woman from the kitchen told us that if we gave her some oats, she would make us hot oatmeal. We obliged, and had hot meals two days in a row.

Mrs. Rakowska appeared as we finished eating.

"Since we left our camp, I estimate we have seen about ten thousand deportees," Jozef told her. "Since we received the word later than most, I would say even more deportees passed through before us. Yet I have not seen any sort of assistance from the Soviet government. Nor have I seen any international relief organization."

"Not to mention all the bodies we have seen along the way," added Kaz.

"It's a tragedy of historic proportions," she said. "The army estimates that about one and a half million Poles were deported from their homes to Siberia. So far, I would say several hundred thousand at the most have made it to the army."

"Where are the others?" I asked.

"They are either like you, still trying to make it out, or they perished," she said. "The Soviets only give assistance directly to the army and to the orphanages. They will not help anyone else. They see everyone else as a potential threat."

"Does the army have lists of those who made it?" Stefan asked. "We all have relatives we are looking for."

"They must have lists of soldiers, I am sure," she replied. "I doubt if they have lists of civilians. That would be impossible."

"Were you in a camp, too?" asked Jozef.

"Yes, north of Perm. We were west of most camps, and one of the first ones to be released." She rose. "Well, let me call and see if the truck and permit have been arranged."

"You have a telephone?" Kaz asked in surprise.

"Yes. Excuse me." She left the room.

\*\*\*

We received a permit for all of us to travel by train to Buzuluk, and a paper concerning the children that we were to present to the orphanage when we arrived. Mrs. Rakowska said we'd travel about three hundred miles from Chistopol. She gave us provisions for three days, but the rations were children's portions. She apologized for not giving us more food, but we didn't complain. We told her we still had some oats, and now they were milled.

They loaded us on a Soviet truck—I was not sure if it was a militia or army truck. The driver wore a Russian uniform. The truck had a canvas roof that was open at one end, but the temperature was much warmer than we were used to, so we weren't worried.

The last time I'd been in any motorized vehicle was when the NKVD took me away from my home. Prior to the deportation, I sometimes rode in my uncle's car. There were not many cars in the Grodna region and my father didn't care much for cars. He loved horses, and that was how we moved about at home—in a carriage in the summer and a sled in the winter. He would sometimes watch as my uncle tinkered with the engine of his car. He would shake his head and say, "Who needs this? It is nothing but trouble."

The truck followed a dirt road not covered by snow. We passed countless deportees walking to Chistopol. When we arrived at the station, the driver didn't even bother to get out of the truck. I lowered the tailgate for the children and hopped out myself. The station looked very familiar—Polish deportees were everywhere, and many looked like they were on their last legs.

The workers at the station were impressed by our official Soviet document and let us board without difficulty. Twelve hours later, the train left for Buzuluk.

\*\*\*

The ride was boring and we were hungry. The oats were all gone.

"What does your house look like, your house in Poland?" Kaz asked me to pass the time.

"It's very old," I said. "It has been in the family for generations."

"What does it look like?"

"It's a country house. About fifteen rooms; the downstairs has a dining room, the kitchen, a maid's room, a drawing room. There's a library, and my father's study."

"Did you have a maid?"

"No. The family used to have a maid, and someone to take care of the horses. But that was a long time ago, before I was born. We played in the maid's room when we were little. I used to hide there when I was mad at my parents."

"You have a coat of arms in the entrance hall?" he asked.

"I think so."

"Sounds like you have a Georgian villa," Kaz said matter-of-factly.

"I guess," I said.

"Miss the lakes?" asked Kaz.

"It's not so much the lakes," I replied. "We didn't go to the lakes that much. I miss the streams and the rivers." I had completely forgotten about the streams until Kaz brought it up. My brother and I had spent our summers at the streams that broke through the endless pines and spruces on our property. The trees provided cool and shady canopies on hot summer days. But it was the summer nights Stan and I spent at the streams that I'd liked the most.

There was an air of mystery in a night in the woods by a stream, but dawn was the best part. Hearing howls at night was terrifying fun. We never heard about anyone being attacked by wolves, not even from the elders, but the howling still made me shiver. I would hear the strangest noises right before dawn, but Stan always knew what they were. He would think for a second and then whisper "wild boar" or "woodcock."

One summer, Stan amazed me when we were fishing with my father. We heard a few distant bird calls and Stan said they were geese.

"In midsummer?" my father asked. "No, no, it is much too early for geese."

Sure enough, flocks of geese passed over our land a few days later.

"You guys are from Grodno, right?" asked Patryk. "Has it always been Polish?"

Kaz chuckled. "It's been Polish, Lithuanian, Byelorussian, Russian—you name it. But my house has belonged to my family for generations."

"Same here," I said.

"Andrzej, how old are you?" asked Stefan. "You're seventeen, right?"

"Yeah."

"When's your eighteenth birthday?"

"In September," I said.

"You know they won't—"

"I know, I know," I said. "I have to tell them I'm eighteen."

Stefan was worried they would not let me join the army, but I didn't even want to be a soldier. I didn't know if I *had* to join, but I was afraid to ask anyone.

"You really want to be in the army?" Kaz asked.

"Do we have much choice?" I countered.

"As long as they feed me, that's all I care about right now," said Kaz.

Stefan turned to Jozef. "You think they'll let me in? You know, with my leg?"

"You walked over three hundred miles," said Jozef. "We will all testify to it. If they don't let you in, they're crazy."

"What was Tomek talking about in the camp?" I asked. "He said something about the Soviets using us as cannon fodder."

Jozef answered, "It's what they call those sent on the assignment that's likely to result in heavy casualties. It's the assignment that nobody wants but somebody's got to do."

"That will be us, for sure," said Kaz. "Something to look forward to."

"Jozef said this general—Anders, is it?—he won't allow it," said Stefan.

"It may not be up to him," warned Patryk.

"The commander-in-chief is just that," said Jozef. "They need Anders for credibility and once he's in charge, they're stuck. If they relieve him of duty, they may lose their credibility, and then men won't fight unless you put a gun to their heads."

"But if they give him an assignment that's suicidal, he's stuck, right?" asked Stefan.

"He can refuse, but it's risky. They'll put up with some dissent if they're sure he can deliver in the long run. But he has to prove himself first," said Jozef.

"Generals don't care about their men," said Zbyszek the ice fisherman. "They spend their time wining and dining. They don't die in the field."

"You talking about your commander in '39?" asked Jozef.

"For one," said Zbyszek. "They're all the same."

"What makes you think your commander was wining and dining while you were fighting? You have no idea what he was doing, do you?" Jozef retorted.

"I know he screwed up—they all screwed up, big time." said Zbyszek.

"Anders is supposed to be good," said Stefan. "Pilsudski picked him."

"Who cares who picked him? They're all the same," said Zbyszek.

Zbyszek was a funny one. I didn't think he meant what he said. If he met Anders, I was willing to bet he would be the first one to snap to attention.

Kaz lay down with his hands under his head. "How do you know if you've won a battle?" he asked.

Jozef stayed focused on Zbyszek. "Your problem, Zbyszek, is that you don't know why battles are won or lost. Not all battles end in defeat."

"They did for us," said Zbyszek. "And I can't see how this can be better than before, not with the Soviets having their hand in there."

Stefan got up and looked out a crack in the wall. "Who knows what the front looks like," he said. "For all we know, the war may be over."

# Chapter Seven

There they were: Polish soldiers with trucks at the Buzuluk train station. I wanted their food, but I didn't want to put on their uniform.

We told them we had to go to the orphanage and they told us to get in "It's all at the same campsite," they said.

Buzuluk was a poor town; it reminded me of Surgut. Mud covered the streets and the trucks moved at a crawl. We came across only one paved road. The camp was actually scattered throughout the forests near Buzuluk. The headquarters were situated in a red brick building with a Polish flag at its entrance—the first Polish flag I'd seen since before the war broke out.

It suddenly occurred to me that my father and brother could be right in this camp. My heart quickened at the thought; I wanted to leap from the truck and search for them, but we had to find the orphanage and produce the paper we received from Mrs. Rakowska. Jola hugged me when I said good-bye. The other children still seemed numb; they let themselves be led away.

"Let's find the mess hall," Kaz suggested, but he was vetoed by the rest, who wanted to head for the enlistment office. I followed uncomfortably, feeling like I was being swept along, with no choice in whether or not I would join the army. *And if I don't join?* I thought. *What will I do?* Kaz and Stefan and the rest were the only people I knew here. Poland was a long way away.

The enlistment tent was not hard to find; we joined a long line of about a hundred men that stretched from its entrance. Jozef had been scanning the sea of faces for anyone he recognized; he suddenly called out and ran over to a man in uniform.

The man didn't recognize Jozef at first—Jozef still had his beard—but he smiled when he heard Jozef's voice. The two talked as they slowly walked over to us. I noticed his uniform was different than any I had seen. It was neither Polish nor Russian. He appeared to be an officer, but I didn't know how to decipher the rank from his uniform.

"The Germans are on the outskirts of Moscow," said the officer. "They are on the verge of total victory."

*Good,* I thought. Maybe the war would be over and we could all go home.

"Russians or Germans," said Kaz as he heard this. "Pick your poison."

"What about the West?" asked Jozef. "Have they entered the war?"

"Ah, now that's where it gets interesting. Last month, the Japanese bombed an American naval base in Hawaii and the Americans declared war on both Japan and Germany."

Jozef nodded. He had always said the Americans would eventually enter the war. "Has Britain invaded the continent?" he asked.

"Without the Americans? No way," the officer said. "And that's what the Russians desperately need. A two-front war for the Germans."

I stood a couple steps away from them with my hands balled into fists in my pockets. I didn't care about any of this. I wanted to ask the officer how I could look for my father and brother, but I couldn't get the question in.

"Who does Anders report to? The Soviets?" asked Jozef.

"No, no. Anders reports to our government. They're in London. General Sikorski is Prime Minister and Commander-in-Chief. Sikorski appointed Anders to lead the new army and the Soviets agreed."

Stefan poked me. "So we're not under the Soviets. No cannon fodder, Andrzej."

The officer heard Stefan and said, "Stalin already requested that some battalions be sent to the Eastern Front, but General Anders refused. Anders isn't taking any crap from Stalin. He told Stalin the earliest we will be ready to fight is in five months."

"Where's the mess hall?" Kaz interjected.

Jozef and the officer ignored him. "How big is the army?" asked Jozef.

"Sixty thousand, and growing every day," the officer said. "Stalin told Anders that the army is getting too large; Stalin said he only agreed to forty thousand men. But the army just keeps growing; hundreds like you get here every day. We can easily go over a hundred thousand."

The officer reached for his cigarettes. The others stared at the pack; they had not seen tobacco for a long time. It suddenly occurred to him that he was tantalizing them, and offered everyone a cigarette, including me. Kaz and I declined but the others enthusiastically accepted. They inhaled the smoke and coughed horribly.

The officer smiled mildly at their discomfort and continued. "The training in the beginning was terrible. The Soviets ran it, but they didn't know what they were doing. As more and more of us got here, we took over. The Soviets are mostly gone, though the NKVD still spies on us. But that's a different story."

"Is this the only camp?" asked Zbyszek.

"No, there are two others—one in Tatishevo and the other in Totskoe."

"Where are they?" asked Zbyszek.

"They're both a couple of hundred miles to the west," he said. "But that reminds me, you guys got here just in time. In a couple of weeks, the entire army is moving to Uzbekistan, where it will be restructured."

"Uzbekistan?" asked Kaz. "Where the hell is that?"

"A thousand miles to the south," said the officer. "It was Sikorski and Anders' idea. They proposed moving the camp to the south, where it will be warmer and easier to train men, and Stalin agreed. The tents here are terrible and it's so cold some men have died of exposure. And there's the disease, too— dysentery, typhoid fever, anything you can think of. We have to get out of here."

The officer paused and glanced around furtively before whispering to Jozef, "There's a rumor that we may go under control of the British Army. They're in Iran and that's right next to Uzbekistan."

Jozef's eyes widened. "The whole army?"

"Yes. Stalin, Sikorski, and Anders have all been talking to Churchill for months. The rumor is that Churchill made a deal with Stalin for Anders' Army to go under British control; the British want to free up their troops from the oil fields in the Middle East and send them to the front. We would replace them in guarding the oil fields."

Kaz had been shifting from one foot to another as they spoke. Now he blurted, "Where can I get something to eat?"

The officer stared at Kaz.

"How's the food here?" asked Stefan.

"Lousy," the man said. "All they have is rice. Not only is it bad, but they keep decreasing the size of the rations. Stalin continues to send us rations for forty thousand men even though our numbers are increasing. He refuses to send more."

He dropped his cigarette to the ground and, as he extinguished it with his boot, added, "And then there are the refugees: women with children, and orphans. They keep coming in and we don't have the food to feed them all."

"How can I check if my family is here?" I finally asked. "My father is a colonel—he must be here."

He hesitated for a second. "Well, you can check the books for enlistees, but that's the other thing—the officers have not reported to the army yet. The only soldiers from the army of '39 who have made it down here so far are privates, corporals, and some lieutenants, like Jozef. But none of the higher ranked officers have made it down—no captains, colonels, or majors."

"Where are they?" asked Jozef.

"The Soviets keep telling Anders that all Polish deportees have been released, including the officers. They tell him that either the officers are in transit or they have fled to another country. They claim there are reports of a large number of officers fleeing to Manchuria. Manchuria! Can you believe it? What bullshit. The Russians are holding our officers so they don't get in the way of their plans. It's obvious."

"I heard the officers are being held in Kozielsk," I said.

"That's right, but there are supposed to be officers in two other camps, as well," he said.

As the officer shook hands with Jozef and left, I could think of nothing more bizarre than my father escaping to Manchuria—wherever that was.

The line of men continued to shuffle forward, until finally our group entered the enlistment tent. After they checked our deportation papers, three officers interviewed each candidate. Only one of the three that interviewed me paid attention to what I said. The others were preoccupied with some order they'd received and didn't like. The attentive officer was probably the oldest. He had eyebrows so bushy, I couldn't help staring at them.

I was nervous at the beginning, and he told me to relax. "It is just an interview," he said, "not an interrogation."

He went through my name, place of birth, schooling, and other basics. I told him I'd turned eighteen years old in November. I told him about my father. I told him about the camp and the trip here. He asked me questions about the others I traveled with. He went through each person, one by one, but he asked the most questions about Jozef.

When I told him Jozef was a lieutenant in the old Polish Army, all three laughed and said they already knew that. I told them how Jozef had helped me in the labor camp, how he led us through the blizzard on the way to Surgut, and how he led us to Surgut by following the moss. I told them he'd told me to find a guardian for the orphans, and that he and Stefan had stolen a sack of oats to feed us all. I told them how Patryk gave up his watch so Jozef could sneak us onto the Trans-Siberian train.

He then asked me why I wanted to join the army.

The question caught me off guard. I'd finally found out that I didn't have to join the army, but it was too late now. "I want to go home," I found myself saying.

He shook his head and said, "We all do."

After about half an hour, they told me that, pending physical examination, I qualified for enlistment. They revealed that some of the others had told them I was instrumental in helping get the orphans to the camp, and they thanked me. The praise from the others gave me a small thrill of pleasure.

The doctor performing the physical read aloud a list of diseases and asked me if I had ever had any of them. I didn't think he was even listening to my answers.

"Do you have lice?" he asked me.

"No."

He checked my scalp and skin and listened to my heart. He took me to an eye chart and had me read the letters, and that was it; the physical was over.

"You passed," he told me, then turned away and called, "send in the next one."

I was issued underwear, a uniform, hat, coat, gloves, and real boots. I learned that the uniforms came from Britain. They distributed the uniforms right next to the showers.

I took my first shower in months. The water was cold, but if felt great anyway. There was real soap, and I inhaled deeply as I lathered up, savoring that soap smell I had forgotten after so long. Our tattered clothes were tossed onto a heap of other burning rags. As I watched mine burn, I felt a twinge of sadness; even if they were only rags, they had saved my life.

The other men cut off their beards and shaved. Kaz looked more or less the same after he shaved, but I couldn't get used to Stefan and Patryk without their beards.

I emerged from the entire enlistment process a soldier: I received a document stating that I was a private of the Polish Forces in the USSR.

Kaz and I found the book containing the names of all the enlistees, but a long line of men waited to look through it. We joined the line and waited about two hours for our turn. The books were divided into two parts. The names in the first part were listed alphabetically. I went through very carefully, afraid I'd miss the name—or perhaps afraid I wouldn't. I saw Barski, Bartek, Borowski, Bronski, but no Bartkowski. I suppressed a surge of disappointment and turned to the second part of the book. Here, the newest enlistees were listed by the dates they'd joined, and it took forever to go through the names one by one. The name Bartkowski didn't appear anywhere. My brother and father were not in the camp.

Kaz couldn't find his father's name, either. "They're not here," he said quietly. "They're not here. Come on, let's go."

I followed numbly behind Kaz, not caring where he led me. I didn't know where they'd taken my brother, Stan, but my father had to have been in a camp not far from Buzuluk. He should have been here by now. I remembered Jozef's friend saying that none of the officers were here yet. I did not know whether this was good or bad. But I knew that the entire army was moving to Uzbekistan in a few weeks, and that was all the time my father and brother had to get down here.

*** 

They let Stefan enlist without any argument. It turned out he was not the first one to enlist with some sort of handicap; many of the men had lost toes from frostbite. I guess the army figured if you could make it down here, you could fight in a battle.

Kaz and I were in the same squad. Our commander, Corporal Jan Plesik, was about twenty-five years old and had been a foot soldier in the old army. He seemed like a decent fellow, as did Marian and Jerzy. Tall, thin Marian had been in a coal mining camp. He was about twenty years old, a university student, before being arrested. Like me, he looked for his family every day. Jerzy was in his thirties. He had been a court stenographer in the High Court of my home town of Grodno.

The others in our squad did not talk much; they seemed depressed.

Stefan and Patryk were in different squads and platoons, but we were all in the same company.

A squad consisted of seven to fourteen soldiers led by a corporal or a sergeant. Three or four squads made a platoon, which was led by a lieutenant. Two or more platoons formed a company, led by a captain or a major. Two or more companies formed a battalion, and on it went.

Jozef, who was made a captain and put in charge of an entire company, insisted we call him Jozef and not Captain Bronski. I guessed we were Siberian blood brothers forever.

They gave us four days to recuperate from our journey before we started basic training; it was hardly enough time. Since men arrived daily, basic training went on nonstop and we joined the course in progress.

I hated basic training. I was forced to learn things I'd always tried to avoid; all the things that used to interest Stan so much. I performed my duties reluctantly, telling myself I was really here to look for my family, and the training was a necessary evil, no more.

Reveille sounded at five. That didn't bother me as much as it had in the prisoner camp—perhaps because, even though I had little say in the matter, I wasn't a prisoner this time. We made our beds and washed and sat down to eat by 5:30. Starting at six, we marched until sunrise, which came at about nine a.m. Then we attended classes on hand-to-hand combat and bayonet assault.

At one p.m. we had lunch, followed by rifle marksmanship, which progressed very slowly because there were not many real rifles and we had to take turns shooting. The Soviets didn't even have real rifles for all of us—we trained with wooden imitations. In the afternoon we had field training exercises followed by more marching, then dinner at seven p.m. As Jozef's friend had said, the meals consisted mostly of rice. Others complained, but I remembered what it had been like in the prisoner camp, and considered the army rations much better than anything I'd had in a long time.

I found the training onerous enough, but I was also ordered to help with the orphans. I just couldn't get away from them. No doubt my experience with the orphans during our journey here prompted the order. It turned out General Anders was fanatical about education. So, twice a week for two hours in the afternoon, I was excused from exercises to teach the older children to read and write.

Mrs. Karska, who was in charge of the orphanage, seemed to think I was her servant. I didn't mind when she asked me to lift this and fix that, but she never looked at me when she asked me to do something. She only pointed at what she wanted done, and looked away as if I'd done something wrong and it was my responsibility to fix the problem.

I reported to Miss Patyk, who had been a schoolteacher in Poland. She was about ten years older than me; thin and very nervous. The children didn't pay much attention to me, but they seemed to overwhelm her. She constantly muttered to herself. Most of the children didn't play. Numbed by their experiences, they showed no emotion.

Not all the children were orphans. Some women left their children in the orphanage simply because they could not feed them. Widowed men brought in others. They entered the army and left their children; they had no other choice.

It was something to see new arrivals in the camp reunited with their children in the orphanage. Sometimes a mother had lost her child in a train station somewhere in Siberia. Or parent and child had been separated back in Poland, before Siberia. In those cases, the workers in the orphanage warned the parent that the child would be unrecognizable—not because the child had grown, but because malnutrition and disease may have altered the child's appearance.

"Don't look for your child," the workers instructed. "Just walk around the orphanage. Let them recognize you." And they were correct; every so often, an adult just stood in front of a group of children and from within the group we heard "Mommy!" or "Daddy!" and a little one ran up to the parent.

After witnessing such reunions, I realized I was much more than a mere baby-sitter, and the duty of helping with the orphans no longer seemed as burdensome as it once had.

As I grew accustomed to my new surroundings, I discovered the rules here were the rules of home—the fair rules of my father and my schoolmaster, rather than the rules of the camp guards in Siberia. Here, I was expected to do my job, but when a dispute arose, the truth mattered more than who was stronger, or who would benefit the most from the situation.

One day Stefan and I helped another company move artillery. A man in that company was one of the first arrivals— he'd been here even before Anders. As we loaded parts of a gun onto a truck, he told us about the first days in Buzuluk.

"In the beginning, we drilled in rags," he told us. "Some wore the remnants of their Polish uniforms from '39. I didn't even have shoes. Most of us just drilled with rags on our feet." He paused. "When the priests got here, they held a mass. I am not a religious man, but even I…" He sighed. "It was quite a sight."

"What do you mean?" Stefan asked.

He hefted a fuse-setting device onto the truck and straightened, stretching tired muscles in his back before replying. "Men cried, especially the soldiers from the old army," he said. "We had just gotten out of the labor camps. I guess the men thought they would never celebrate mass again. You know that hymn, *Our Free Country Give Back to Us, Oh Lord?* They sang that. Even I thought it was something."

I remembered that hymn. I'd heard it in church, but I'd never thought about the words before. I realized the hymn must have been from before the Great War.

"When did Anders get here?" Stefan asked.

"A few weeks after me. We marched for him when he got here," the man said. "He didn't want us to, but we insisted. We may have been half starved, but we were clean-shaven and showered. We wanted to show the Soviets how a real army behaves." His eyes grew distant. "I remember Anders saluted us, but he just kept staring at our foot rags."

"When did you start to get supplies?" I asked.

The man shook his head slightly, jarred out of the memory by my question. "The supplies? A couple of months later. The supplies came from the British. It was part of the deal they made with the Soviets."

\*\*\*

We looked around and asked others, but no one had seen anyone else from our camp in Siberia. We found it hard to believe that all of them had died in the blizzard. One day, we sat down and tried to reconstruct what had happened.

"We separated from the others twice," said Kaz. "The first time was before the storm."

"Yes, that's right," I said. "The first separation occurred our first night out. One group stopped to camp for the night, but we continued."

"That's because Kalinski hated the men from Barrack Four," said Kaz. "He's the one who said we should keep going. He saw they stopped and he talked us into going on."

"I didn't know that," I said.

"It doesn't matter who liked who," said Stefan. "What matters is the second separation. We left when the blizzard started. We left them in the valley, right?"

"Right," I said.

"How long would you say we walked in the blizzard before we found woods?" asked Stefan.

"It couldn't have been more than twelve, fourteen hours," said Kaz.

"Yeah, about that," I agreed.

"So we left about a hundred men in the valley during the blizzard," said Stefan. "The blizzard went on for about four days. They were only a twelve-hour walk from woods. It is almost impossible for all of them to have died of exposure. Even if some stayed there during the entire storm, at least some would have left."

"But you can't assume they went in the same direction as us," I said. "Maybe we were lucky. Maybe the only woods for miles lay in the direction we took. Still, what about that group we separated from the first night? The ones Kalinski didn't like. Where did they go? Do you think they were in the valley when the blizzard hit?"

"Who knows," said Stefan. "They are not here now, I can tell you that." Frowning, he rose and paced in the confines of the tent. "That's the part I don't get," he said. "How could *all* of them perish?"

"Maybe they couldn't get the wood to burn," I said. "God knows, I still can't get a fire started with that flint rock."

Stefan stopped pacing and lifted a skeptical brow at me. "But *all* of them?"

"Maybe they got to Surgut but there were no more trains," suggested Kaz. "Maybe there was a train wreck. Maybe the Soviets decided no more Poles would be allowed on the Trans-Siberian Railway. Who knows?" He dropped his voice. "This wouldn't have happened if Kalinski wasn't so stubborn. He was obsessed with those markers—he should have been more flexible. I don't know why they all listened to him. He must have been a soldier," Kaz mused. "I bet you he was an officer or something."

"Oh, yes," said Stefan. "He was an officer in the army of '39."

"I knew it!" yelled Kaz.

"The Soviets thought he was a lieutenant," said Stefan, "but he had false papers. He held a higher rank than that—that's why Jozef always listened to him."

"How high??" asked Kaz. "Was he a general, or something?"

"I don't know; Jozef wouldn't tell me. He still won't tell me, if I ask him now. That subject is off-limits. I don't even think Kalinski was his real name."

\*\*\*

There were Roman Catholic, Orthodox, Jewish, and Protestant chaplains in the camp. Some came out of the camps of Siberia and others came from England, with the assistance of the British government. I wanted to attend mass, but I first went to confession. For the first time in almost two years, I came in contact with a priest.

"Bless me father, for I have sinned," I said as I entered the booth. "It has been two years since my last confession."

He asked me if I had anything to confess.

"I lied about my age to get into the army," I said.

"How old are you?" he asked.

"I will be eighteen next month."

"Did you steal food or money from others?"

"We stole a sack of oats on our trip down here. We were running out of food."

"Who did you steal it from?"

"From a freight train at a station in Siberia."

"Hardly a sin," he said. "Did you steal food or money from another person when you were in Siberia?"

"No," I said.

"Were there others you could have helped but didn't, because you were only thinking about yourself?" he asked. "I ask, because the guilt for that will only increase with time. Sooner or later, you have to come to terms with it."

"There were some in the prison camp I could have helped, but I didn't. Some of the men in my barrack were too weak to work and did not get their bread cards. I could have given them some of my bread, but there wasn't even enough for me."

The priest didn't respond. I heard his fingers tapping on the arm of his chair.

"Tell me, father," I said. "Why has God done this? Why did he send all of us to Siberia?"

"This was not done by God," he quickly answered. "Oh, no. This was done by men who ignore God and his laws."

I heard his chair creak as he changed position.

"You see, young man, Germany and Russia are stricken with a plague that is much worse than even typhus or smallpox. This plague is a belief that man can create a world without God and His principles. Those who are infected think that, in order to create a new world, they must destroy the old one. Villages, towns, and nations—all must be liquidated, they think. But when it comes time to build their new world, they realize that nothing lasting can be built without God's principles. They cannot admit this to themselves, so they continue to blame others for their failures. Entire ethnic groups and nations are blamed and persecuted. The destruction continues until there is nothing left."

"But as with every plague, not all of those exposed become ill. Some keep a clear mind and stay true to their principles. These chosen people are not of one nation. They are scattered everywhere. They are not recognizable to those who destroy and are not even seen as a threat. In the end, the destroyers will destroy themselves and those with clear minds will rebuild society according to the rules of God."

"But why does God let it happen?" I asked.

"God's justice sometimes comes slowly," he answered. "But it always comes. In the end, it always arrives. That, I am sure of."

"But so many people have already died," I said. "I have seen countless dead on my way from Siberia."

He stopped tapping his fingers and did not respond.

"Pray," he finally said. "Pray, my son, that this plague will soon end. It is not the first, nor the last epidemic."

"And my penance?"

"Pray for all the souls who died in Siberia," he said, and closed the window.

\*\*\*

When Stefan told me of a man in his platoon from my town who recognized my name, I quickly sought him out. I knew the man; I didn't know his name, but I knew his face. He knew my father; he lived in the town of Grodno itself, and he used to deliver coal to our house. He was also an assistant to our parish priest, and he thought that was why the Soviets sent him and his family to Siberia. He told me he knew for a fact that my father was sent to the camp in Kozielsk.

"I was already on the Russian trains," he said, "The ones with the wide tracks. We stopped at the station in Kozielsk. They opened the doors and there was some confusion, because a train on an adjacent track was unloading men onto the same platform. The guards quickly tried to separate us from the others. I heard them say, 'No, no, they're with a different group. This is their destination. You are continuing.' And that's when I saw your father. He was among those they said were staying at Kozielsk."

This was the closest I'd been to any member of my family for over two years. My heart pounded as though my father was more than another man's recollection; as though he was here, somewhere, in the flesh. I suddenly yearned for my family with an intensity that frightened me a little. *He's not here,* I reminded myself. *And he should be.*

"Are you sure it was him?" I asked.

"I am one hundred percent certain," he said emphatically. "Like I see you right now."

"Did he see you? Did you talk?"

"He didn't see me, but I saw him," he said as he pulled a cigarette from his pocket and tapped it on the tabletop. "There was no way I could have approached him. The guards wouldn't have allowed it."

"So what happened next?"

"They led us away to another platform, another train. That was the last I saw him." He paused and lit the cigarette before continuing. "But I will never forget what the guard said: 'They are stopping here. This is their destination.'"

"So you continued east?" I asked.

"Oh yes, way east—we traveled for another month on those trains."

"How long ago was this?"

"They don't want to let them out," he said. "The Soviets don't want to deal with the officers. They know the officers would not put up with any of their crap. What a bunch of bastards."

"How long ago?" I pressed.

"Let me see, this was at the very beginning of the war." He frowned in concentration as he rolled the tip of his cigarette in the ashtray. "It was still fall. Yes, the fall of '39."

"Did you see my brother?"

"I'm sorry, but I didn't recognize you when you came in, and I would not have recognized your brother, either. Young people change quickly. But there were no young men on his train. I didn't know it then, but your father was among other officers. He was the only one I recognized."

I thanked him. Now I knew beyond doubt where they'd sent my father. But why wasn't he here?

\*\*\*

Three weeks passed and there was still no sign of anyone from my family. The anticipation I'd felt while talking to the man from my hometown had long since faded. Now, as the entire camp packed up and departed for Uzbekistan, I worried that my father would never find me, that I'd never see any of them again.

I and ten other soldiers were ordered to help with the orphans during the journey. We would be traveling over one thousand miles, by both train and truck.

As they had on my trip to Buzuluk, the trains frequently stopped in the middle of nowhere and we sometimes waited several days before continuing. Thousands of half-starved refugees followed the army. I talked to the soldiers and the other deportees, and as I listened to their stories, I started to realize the scope of what the Soviets had done to Poland, how systematically they had drained the Polish nation.

It took three weeks to reach Uzbekistan, a dry land of vast, sandy plains alternating with cotton fields and deserts. The warm weather made my coat unnecessary. The army settled in near a town called Tashkent. The camp consisted of primitive huts and many tents. As soon as we arrived, the officers searched the headquarters and found electronic listening devices planted by the NKVD. These were promptly destroyed. There'd been similar devices in Buzuluk, I learned.

Every day, hundreds—if not thousands—of refugees arrived. All were malnourished, hungry, and exhausted; many were sick and died soon after their arrival. The army couldn't feed them all; Stalin continued to provide rations for forty thousand despite the fact that the army now numbered close to seventy-five thousand.

The Soviet officials told the refugees to disperse into the local collective farms known as kolhzozes. But word went around quickly that the Uzbeg people were themselves dying of starvation on the farms, and the refugees tried to stay close to the army. The Soviet militia then tried to force the refugees onto the farms. The refugees turned to the army for protection, but the army had no food or shelter for them.

Some of the refugees built huts from clay and straw. The only fuel they could find was cow dung, which didn't provide enough heat to boil water. The water couldn't be sterilized, so the epidemics continued to spread. Relief packages started to arrive from America. They helped, but there was simply not enough to meet the demand. If the situation continued, most of the refugees would die. Unfortunately, that may have been exactly the result the Soviets intended.

Rumors flew around the camp: the Soviets were trying to starve us to death. No, others said, they were not doing this on purpose; things were really bad in the Soviet Union. Their counteroffensive near Moscow was successful and they pushed the Germans back, but they were still on the brink of capitulation.

For me, there was one silver lining to this situation: as long as refugees continued to come in, there was still hope my family would make it here.

I grew weak from lack of food. Finally, the army decided to stop our physical training. Men were simply too weak, and the officers feared that too much discipline would decrease morale even further. We just sat around all day and played cards, waiting for the supply trucks to arrive.

We were informed that the fate of the army was under negotiation, and again the rumors ran rampant. Many said we would go Iran and under British command.

Jozef was against this. "As much as I don't like it," he said, "we must stay side by side with the Soviets. If we go under British command, we will fall under their agenda. But if we are with the Soviets, we'll be there when they enter Poland. We must be there if we want to reclaim Poland."

Not long afterward came the announcement many were waiting to hear. Three of the army's six divisions were transferring to Iran under the leadership of the British. The divisions were not at our site; they were in Tatishevo and Totskoe. The men there must have been excited, but the rest of us wondered what it meant for us. We were told not to worry; it was only a matter of time before the rest of the army left the Soviet Union. Men were still apprehensive; no one wanted to be left behind.

"General Anders is staying right with you," the officers tried to reassure us. "He will not leave without you."

As civilians heard of the departure, they converged on the army. Many women and children traveled with the first wave to Iran. Those who couldn't get on board a train traveled on foot.

Some Soviet officials didn't want to let them cross into Iran, but they had no choice; the refugees had their deportation papers. On surrender of their deportation papers at the border, the refugees were told that they were forbidden to tell anyone about their experiences in the Soviet Union.

Several weeks after the three divisions departed, the rest of us learned we were leaving for Iran as well. We would take trucks to the port of Krasnovodsk, then travel over the Caspian Sea to Iran. Most of the men were ecstatic. Some thought it was too good to be true, to be finally leaving Russia.

"We are finally heading back to civilization," said Kaz.

The night after the announcement, I dreamt of my father again. We were fishing by our stream, and he was teaching me to cast. He told me how important it was to be patient when fishing. "Patience is hope," he said. But he did not give me instructions on what I should do, as he had in the last dream.

The water in the stream was more turbulent than I'd ever remembered it being, even after a downpour. *It doesn't matter how patient you are*, I thought in the dream, *the fish can't even make it to the bait.* The fish were being pulled downstream.

I woke up in a cold sweat and remembered that we were leaving for Iran.

* * *

I'd been ordered to help the orphanage with their evacuation, but when I arrived, I found a distressed Miss Patyk in conversation with Mrs. Karska, the director of the orphanage.

"When did she call?" asked Mrs. Karska.

"This morning, and again now," said Miss Patyk.

"Did you tell the major?"

"Yes," Miss Patyk replied. "He told me to tell her to get the kids here, and we will take them with us. But now she tells me she can't even get trucks."

"What happened?" I asked.

95

Miss Patyk sat down and started biting her nails. "Oh it's terrible, Andrzej, just terrible," she said. "There's an orphanage about two hundred miles from here, in Karshi. Mrs. Sokolnicka runs it. She telephoned our orphanage and asked us for help. The Soviets want to liquidate her orphanage."

"It's her own fault," said Mrs. Karska. "She should have been nicer to the Delegatura."

"The Soviets want to send the children to the collective farms in the area," Miss Patyk continued. "There is no way the children would survive very long on those farms, but the Soviets don't care."

"She always acted like she didn't need the Delegatura," sniffed Mrs. Karska. "Always too proud, always cursing the Communists. And what did it get her?"

Mrs. Patyk looked at her. "The Delegatura is not a Communist organization."

"The Delegatura? They're supposed to help with the orphans, right?" I asked.

"Yes," said Miss Patyk. "Mrs. Sokolnicka had been under their protection. But the Soviets just came in and ordered her to disperse the children."

"Well, where is the Delegatura? Won't they help?"

"She can't find them anywhere," Miss Patyk told me.

"They must be around," said Mrs. Karska. "They are avoiding her on purpose."

"Can't the children come here?" I asked.

"The major said it's okay, but now Mrs. Sokolnicka tells me that, without the help of the Delegatura, she has no trucks."

"Why can't we go and get them?" I asked.

"That's not how it works, young man," said Mrs. Karska. "The army does not send trucks hundreds of miles in search of children. That's the Delegatura's job."

"This isn't a search," said Miss Patyk abruptly. "It's a simple transport."

Mrs. Karska looked away, dismissing our arguments. "If you don't get along with the people in power, it comes back to haunt you."

"The army is in charge," said Miss Patyk. "It's a Polish army and these are Polish children."

"If the army's in charge, why can't we feed all the children?" asked Mrs. Karska. "And who's going to feed all *those* children, if they come here?"

"Jozef!" I exclaimed. "He's a captain who helped me bring orphans down here from Siberia; I'll tell Jozef about the situation. I'm sure he will help."

"Go and try, Andrzej," said Miss Patyk. "Make him realize how important this is. Those kids will die if they're sent to the collectives—this is their last chance to make it out of here. Let him know that."

I ran over to Jozef's office and when I was admitted, I quickly outlined the situation; he agreed that we had to do everything we could to prevent the orphans from landing in the kolhkozes. He told me he would speak to his superiors.

Later that afternoon, he called for me and said he'd arranged for four trucks to transport the orphans here first thing in the morning. He had orders to send an armed escort and three soldiers to assist, including me.

We headed out on the dusty, bumpy roads and made it to Karshi in just over six hours. The orphanage was overcrowded, just like ours, and the children looked at us with the same empty stare. Mrs. Sokolnicka was relieved to see us, but still worried that the Soviet militia would intervene.

"We have a squad of armed men," I told her. "No one will stop us."

"Until you arrived, I'd even considered marching the orphans the two hundred miles to your campsite on foot," she admitted sheepishly. "I guess I was panicking."

We decided the children would fit in two trucks and the other two would carry belongings, cots, and supplies. About to load boxes onto one of the trucks, I saw that the others had already loaded the cots, and now there wasn't enough space left for the boxes.  I tried to stack them for a few minutes, but abandoned the attempt and decided to remove the cots and start all over.

As I stacked the cots on the ground next to the truck, a little boy came up to me and tugged insistently on my pants.

"This is no place for you, here," I said.  "Better get back inside, before you get hurt."

He kept tugging.

"Andrzej."

I reached into the truck for another cot.  Many of the cots were old and did not fold down like they were supposed to. *This will double the amount of space they take in the truck,* I thought, and I tried to force the old hinges to move.

"Andrzej," the boy said again.

As I pushed at a rusted hinge, I absently absorbed the voice. The voice was before Siberia.  It was before trains and fish head stew, before snow banks and dead bodies in the snow.

I looked down and stared at the boy's narrow face, noticing how the skin hung from it, noticing lips cracked from scurvy. But his eyes... his eyes—Jesus Christ, it was Michal!  It was my brother Michal.

Still staring at him, I slowly placed my hand on top of his head to see if he was real.  "Michal," I whispered.  "Michal, it's me, Andrzej."

I squatted down and stared into his eyes.  Those were the eyes that used to spy on me from the space below the piano in the parlor.  Those eyes searched our stream for frogs and the kitchen pantry for chocolate.  They monitored the den window endlessly to make sure the squirrels did not get into the birdhouse. Those were the eyes that were trying to understand why they took dad away and why we had to leave our home.

I grabbed him and held him tightly.  I started to gasp in spasms.

I picked him up.  I held him in my arms and squeezed his chest against mine.  I don't know how long I held him.  It was as though he had a magical energy that filled me as I held him. I could feel it flowing into me in strong currents.

"Are dad and Stan with you?" he asked. "Mom said we would find all three of you."

I held him away and looked into his face. "Where's mom?"

"Are you a soldier?" he asked. "Soldiers helped us move here. Are you a soldier?"

"Is mom with you?"

"Mom got the fever."

"Where is she?"

"She's in the field by the lake."

*Oh God, oh God*... "What field?" I asked him, even though I didn't want to know.

"The field where they buried her."

Still gasping back sobs, I started to walk with him in my arms. I walked and turned and walked as if we were lost in a cave and looking for a way out. I wanted to run away with him but there was nowhere to go.

I saw the truck and carried him over and sat him down on the tailgate. I gazed into his eyes. Michal showed no emotion. He wore a blank expression and his mouth hung slightly open. He looked just like the other children.

"What happened to mom?" I asked in a low voice.

He did not answer. He rubbed his nose and sighed.

"She got a fever?"

He nodded. "Mrs. Majska gave her lots of soup, but it didn't help."

"Did she get sick in the camp?"

"Yeah. She had a fever like the other women."

"Did she die in the camp?"

"The men buried her in a field by the lake. They put a cross on the grave and they said prayers."

"In the camp?"

"Yeah."

"Who took care of you after that?"

99

"Mrs. Majska. She gave me potatoes, but saved the bread for her kids."

"Where is Mrs. Majska?"

He shrugged. "Mom said we would find all of you. Is dad with you?"

I put my hand on his head. "No Michal, they aren't with me. But we will find them."

Michal looked very malnourished. His lips told me he had not had any greens for a long time. The camp he'd been in couldn't have been much better than mine.

"What happened to Mrs. Majska?" I asked him.

"She got the fever too."

"Where is she?"

"They buried her in the field, like mom. Are you a soldier?"

"Yes Michal, I am. And we are leaving. We are going away where it will be better," I said firmly.

"You mean Iran?" he asked. "Mrs. Sokolnicka said we have to go to Iran."

"Yes, that's right, Iran." *For now,* I told myself.

"Is that where they are? Dad and Stan?"

*Were they?* I wondered. Had they been in Tatishevo or Totskoe, and were now on their way to Iran with the first three divisions? I turned to Mrs. Sokolnicka as she slowly walked up to us.

"You found a relative?" she asked.

"He's my brother," I said.

She nodded and folded her arms; she had seen this scene before.

Michal told Mrs. Sokolnicka, "My brother's a soldier."

"Who brought him here?" I asked her.

"Let's see... he came here about a month ago. A man brought him, a man who was joining the army. He had three of his own children and Michal. I don't remember his name."

"Are dad and Stan in Iran?" asked Michal.

"I hope so," I said. "We will look for dad and Stan together, Michal."

"I think I know what children Michal came with," she said. "I can check the name for you."

"Thank you. And thank you for taking care of my brother."

She smiled and turned away. "I have more boxes for you when you're ready," she said as she walked toward a tent.

She was a very kind woman, very different from what Mrs. Karska described. *As always, you have to consider the source,* I thought. I looked at my brother. "Are you hungry, Michal?"

"No, I had a bowl this morning. Do you have a gun?"

He didn't show emotion, but at least he showed interest and asked questions, which was better than some of the other children I had seen.

"Yes, Michal, but you can't play with it. Why don't you watch me load the truck? From now on, we will stay together, okay?"

"Okay."

Michal never took his eyes from me as I struggled with the cots. I asked him more about the camp he and mom had been in, but his responses were fragmented. From what I could make out, Michal and my mother were in a posiolek near a large lake. Mom worked in the woods and it sounded like Michal stayed in a schoolroom during the day. Some sort of epidemic had swept through the camp and many of the women fell sick. Mom was one of them.

I was glad I had the cots and the boxes to think about.

By the afternoon, we'd finished packing and took off in our trucks. I had Michal by my side. *I have to make sure I get Michal out of this hellhole or he'll perish,* I thought. There should be no problem for us to leave the Soviet Union—I was a soldier and Michal was an orphan—but you never knew, with Satan's system. What if the Soviets changed their minds? What if the British suddenly changed their plans? The faster we got out of here, the better.

*All we have to do is take the trucks to the port of Krasnovodsk on the Caspian Sea,* I assured myself. *Once we get on the ship, we're out of the Soviet Union and they can't touch him.  When I go off to the war, Michal will be in the hands of the British.  They are a civilized people.  They'll have decent schools and provisions.*  The plan was not great, but at least it was a plan.

I realized I was not surprised to learn my mother was dead.  I was beginning to fear they all were.  I glanced at Michal, who watched the road from the seat beside me.  I hoped my mother knew that I had Michal.

# Chapter Eight

"Of course I want to see him," Kaz said.

Around us, ropes were released and tents collapsed, one after another. Cots were folded and stacked into trucks, just like the day before, in Karshi.

"You are the first one to find a relative," he said. "We're not leaving for hours. I want to meet him for good luck."

Kaz and I found Jozef visiting the orphans' tents. At first, I thought he came to see if Mrs. Sokolnicka's children had arrived, but it was much more than that. He was delivering new identification papers for Mrs. Sokolnicka; they were changing her name to Komor-something. The Soviet militia in Karshi had issued a warrant for her arrest after we left. They telephoned the army that morning, asking if she was here, but one of our officers claimed total ignorance.

"I hear you found more than you expected in Karshi," Jozef told me. Mrs. Sokolnicka must have told him about my brother.

"More than I bargained for," I said with a smile.

Jozef was the only officer we could speak with freely and we didn't see him often, so Kaz took advantage of this chance meeting to glean some information. "What's your opinion of all this, Jozef?" he asked. "Why are the Soviets letting us leave?"

Jozef liked to lecture and jumped on the opportunity. "Ah, it's not that simple," he said. "First of all, Anders and Stalin don't even talk to each other anymore. Last month, Stalin told Anders he wanted a division sent immediately to the Russian front. Anders refused, saying they had no training in artillery."

Watching Jozef as he talked to Kaz, I noticed he'd grown a moustache. General Anders wore a moustache.

"Stalin wanted cannon fodder," Kaz concluded.

"He can refuse Stalin, just like that?" I asked.

"Well, he did. And Stalin went nuts and cut our rations. He said he would not send rations for more than forty thousand and any number over that should evacuate to Iran and go under British command."

"So it started at rations for forty thousand and dropped to zero?" asked Kaz.

"Exactly," Jozef replied. "The Americans promised us tons of wheat and we never saw a grain. When Anders asked him about this, Stalin said he hadn't received it yet."

"Is that when the first wave left?" I asked.

Jozef nodded. "Then it got worse when Stalin refused to let Poles transfer here from the Red Army."

"Poles in the Red Army?" I exclaimed. It never occurred to me that Stan could have been in the Red Army.

"When the Soviets invaded, they did not send everyone to Siberia, as they did with us. Thousands, if not hundreds of thousands, were drafted into the Red Army," said Jozef very slowly. "And Anders wants them back."

Michal ran up to me and I scooped what felt like a feather into my arms. I told him to say hello to his uncles. Michal gave them a glance, but that was it. Kaz poked Michal in the stomach but received only a strange look from Michal, as if he wondered why someone would do such a thing.

"They argued about a whole bunch of things," Jozef continued. "Like the officers. They still haven't released the officers and Stalin keeps giving him this nonsense that they fled the country. You know, Anders is one of those Protestants who—"

"Manchuria!" Kaz suddenly yelled, laughing. "Our fathers ran off to Manchuria! They are returning to their Chinese roots!"

Kaz was in one of his moods. When life was beyond his control, he cracked jokes. I favored him with an annoyed glance and then focused on Jozef again. "Anders is a Protestant?" I asked.

"Why is Stalin letting us go under British command?" asked Kaz.

"Well, up until recently, it looked like Stalin wanted us on the front. But he doesn't want our number to be too large."

"Why?" I asked.

"Stalin owes me some American wheat," said Kaz emphatically. "I will not forget this, even after we leave."

"Stalin was afraid if there were several hundred thousand Polish soldiers at the front, we would push the Germans back and reclaim Poland. That is what I was hoping for," said Jozef.

"God forbid having Polish soldiers in Poland," said Kaz.

"So it looked like he wanted some of us on the Eastern Front, but then all of a sudden, out of thin air, Stalin told General Anders that he had no problem with the remaining forces being evacuated to Iran and put under British command."

"Why?"

Michal wiggled. He wanted me to let him down. "Andrzej, when are we leaving for Iran?" he asked.

"After lunch," I said. "After lunch, you and I will get in the truck together."

"You like to ride in trucks?" asked Kaz. Michal didn't answer and Kaz mugged exaggerated disappointment.

"Some say Stalin agreed because he could no longer feed us, but others say that, clearly, Stalin and Churchill struck a deal," Jozef answered.

"What's Churchill's angle?" asked Kaz.

"That's another matter. The British want to make it look like they're taking us for humanitarian reasons. You know, to relieve their guilt for not honoring their agreements with Poland when the Germans invaded."

"Bullshit," said Kaz.

"Exactly," said Jozef. "Churchill has thousands of British troops in the Middle East that he wants to send to the front. But someone has to protect the oil fields of Iran and hold Palestine. And that's where we come in."

"But why does Stalin agree?" I asked.

"The two front war," Kaz said. "Stalin needs the two front war."

I hadn't expected the answer from Kaz. Maybe it was a stupid question.

"Right," said Jozef. "A western front would put pressure on the Germans from both sides, and decrease the burden on the Red Army. But the British troops cannot simply leave the Middle East without replacements. The threat of German control of the region is always there. Churchill does not question our loyalty to the British."

"Who made the agreement for the entire army to leave for Iran?" asked Kaz. "Anders or Sikorski?"

"I don't know," said Jozef. "Some say that General Sikorski wanted part of the army to stay in the Soviet Union so they could one day liberate Poland from the east, and that General Anders made the decision on his own, but no one I know is sure."

"If Sikorski knew how bad the conditions here are, he would agree to evacuate us for sure," said Kaz.

I realized we were totally at the mercy of General Anders' judgment. This was a very complicated situation involving many countries and we were just like little pawns. *Better a pawn in the army than a prisoner in Siberia,* I thought.

"What's Anders like?" I asked. "Do you know him?"

"I don't know him personally, but it's just like I said before we got here. There's nothing phony about him."

"Will the British let him lead?"

"If he can survive the Bolsheviks, he can survive them," Kaz told me.

"Let's put it this way," said Jozef. "When the Soviets invaded Poland, Anders was imprisoned at NKVD headquarters in Moscow and tortured. When the Germans invaded Russia, they released him like they released us; they needed his support to create an army that Poles would believe was legitimate. The British will need him for the same reason."

As Jozef turned to leave, I suddenly remembered about Kalinski. "Did Kalinski ever make it to the army?" I asked.

Jozef raised his eyebrows. "No, he is officially missing."

"I heard that was not his real name," I countered.

"You heard right."

"Was he an officer?"

"You've been talking to Stefan, I see," he said. "Kalinski was a general in the old army. That is all I can tell you. And you didn't hear it from me."

\*\*\*

Now, with Michal to think of, I was eager to help with the orphans on the journey to the port of Krasnovodsk, where we boarded a small ship to cross the Caspian Sea. I had Michal by my side the entire time. We were finally leaving the Soviet Union! But I was still afraid we would be turned back to Russia.

Michal showed some interest in being on a ship. I didn't want him to know about my anxiety and pretended I was excited, as well. We arrived in a port named Pahlevi, but it wasn't until we actually had our feet on Persian soil that I relaxed.

To our surprise, the Persians, many of them children, greeted us. When the Persian children gave candy and gifts to our Polish children, some of the orphanage workers started to cry. I watched Michal for his reaction, wondering if being around other children would draw him out. He put a piece of chocolate in his mouth and quietly ate it. A little Persian boy gave him a stuffed animal; he didn't look at it much, but he held it very tightly, as though afraid it would be taken from him.

Nuns from a convent in Teheran met us and divided the children into several groups. I accompanied Michal's group to a local church, where they would spend the night. I felt my throat tighten when I saw the red brick church, the first church I had seen since before the war. I'd always taken the presence of churches in Poland for granted. I saw it differently now. Houses of worship had to be protected, above all.

The next morning, the children were again divided into two groups and sent to two boarding schools near Teheran—one run by a Protestant English missionary couple, and the other by French Roman Catholic nuns. I accompanied Michal on the bus to the nuns' school.

The nuns were as organized as an army; upon their arrival, the children were washed, disinfected, and given new clothes. I was relieved to see that the school was well kept and the classrooms and dormitories were spacious and clean. *Michal's lips should heal soon,* I thought when I saw the array of food in the kitchens, which included a variety of vegetables and fruits. *Mother would have nothing against me leaving Michal here.*

"You'll like it here very much," I told Michal as we walked in the green gardens surrounding the school. I told him that I had to go back to the army, but I would continue to look for dad and Stan. "Mom's gone to heaven," I said. "Someday, we'll all see her there—we'll all be together again."

He nodded and nodded, but didn't say anything.

"I have to leave now," I told him. "I have to join my company, but I'll be back soon."

"When?" he asked quickly.

"As soon as they let me," I said. "It could be a few days, or a few weeks at the most. But remember, I am not far away. I am nearby, and I will be back for sure."

He nodded again; I hugged him and left.

\*\*\*

The British were prepared to receive our army; they had food, medicine, and supplies, but they had no idea we would arrive in such terrible shape. The men were plagued with malnutrition, vitamin deficiencies, dysentery, and now malaria. The British soldiers didn't say anything, but we could tell they were shocked.

"What did they expect?" Kaz said. "We were in labor camps in Siberia and then traveled thousands of miles to get here."

"Maybe they don't even know what we've been through," said Patryk. "Maybe all they know is that they were to receive an army."

We underwent delousing: our clothes were collected and burned again, as they'd been in Buzuluk. We washed ourselves thoroughly with disinfectant. Many men's heads were shaved. Finally we were issued new uniforms—standard British uniforms with a patch on the shoulder emblazoned with 'Poland.'.

"Why does it have to say 'Poland' in English?" Jerzy grumbled. "Why didn't they write it in Polish?"

"Better 'Poland' in English than 'prisoner' in Russian," replied Kaz.

The Iranian landscape was somewhat similar to Uzbekistan: vast plains and deserts, but there were more mountainous areas. We constructed our campsites with renewed energy. The supplies seemed limitless. Everything was new, even the tents. We were issued new boots, side arms, and rifles.

My rifle was a Lee Enfield Mark No. 4. The soldiers of '39 said it had fantastic bolt action—it was rotating, and could fire up to fifteen rounds per minute. I couldn't get over how heavy the thing was compared to my old wooden rifle.

There was abundant food, and we were warned not to overeat; our stomachs would not take it, we were told. I carefully ate hard-boiled eggs and boiled beef for the first time in almost two years, savoring every bite.

After two weeks, I received a pass to visit Michal.

As I walked through the halls in search of Michal, I could tell the children were eating better, but those I saw weren't playing on their own. There was no joy in their faces.

Michal told me some of the children were going to Africa. *Are we to be separated yet again?* I thought, alarmed. I sought out Sister Catherine, a young and energetic nun I'd met when we'd brought Michal here. Polish was not her first language, but she spoke it fairly well.

Seated on a bench in a small courtyard, she divided her attention between me and a little girl who had a problem with the bow in her hair. "He's telling you the truth," she said. "There is a group heading out for Africa in a few days."

"Why Africa? Haven't these children traveled enough?"

She shrugged, still fussing with the bow. "That's where they have provisions and accommodations."

"Who has accommodations?" I demanded.

"Uganda. It's a British colony. The British colonies offer peace and safety." She fixed the girl's bow and sent her off.

"Why can't they stay here?"

I realized my voice had risen when she looked up sharply, eyes wide. Then they softened; she understood. "We don't have the accommodations here. More families and orphans keep arriving every day. If children have fathers in Anders' Army we try and keep them here, but the others are sent wherever we find placement."

"Will Michal be sent out?" I asked.

She smiled gently and put her hand over mine. "For the children going to Africa, the war with all its painful memories will be over. No more long train rides, no more snow, no more death."

I slid my hand out from under hers. "Is Michal going?"

"It's only a matter of time."

"But Michal has a relative—me. I'm his brother."

"But you are not a parent. Michal is in the group of children who don't have a living parent verified."

I rose abruptly and turned to face her. "Who decides who stays and who goes?"

She sighed and looked at me as if she understood. "Look, I'm sorry, but it's not just the orphans; many families are going as well."

"Will Michal be sent to Africa?"

"Maybe; we don't know. Wherever we find placement."

I paced left; right. How could I stop this? I stopped in front of her again. "I can't let my brother go to Africa."

She held her hands out, palms up. "What do you want us to do? They can't stay here; there isn't enough room or food. It may not be Africa. We are trying to find places for these children in many countries."

If there was an alternative, it didn't come to my mind. It appeared I had little to say in the matter. "When will you know?"

"It's impossible to predict. We will let you know as soon as we do."

\*\*\*

As our strength returned, our training progressed by leaps and bounds. All we had to worry about was our assignments. Complaints were fewer; no one had to worry about bread cards or surviving a frigid night. In fact, the heat could be intense at midday, and it took some time to get used to.

Other companies trained with artillery and armored vehicles, but my company was infantry. We progressed from basic training to more advanced training in concealment, camouflage, fighting positions, movement techniques, observation, communications, and combat intelligence.

I found it difficult to absorb everything I was taught. The exercises and lessons were intense; they were on different levels, but all were interconnected. I had to learn and remember many different things for each activity—things like grip, aim, and breath control in marksmanship, along with positioning, reloading, cleaning, and more. Some activities needed only common sense—natural concealment was better than artificial concealment—but others had to be learned. I learned that, when choosing fighting positions or building foxholes, the field of sector and field of fire had to be kept in mind. Curved foxholes were better in close terrain than straight two-man holes. Infantry fire teams moved in wedge formation; the team leader was at the apex and men spread ten meters apart. Wire communications were more secure than radio and preferable in defensive positions. Intelligence information had to be reported to your leader in a certain order: location, size of the enemy, unit type, and activity. I started to dream about the lessons in my sleep.

Through it all, I visited Michal about once a week.

The men started to ask when they would be sent into battle. They figured the sooner they entered the war, the faster they could help end it and return home.

In Russia, General Anders had established a British-style women's army corps known as the PSK. As this outfit swelled with refugees that followed the army out of Russia, he developed it further. The PSK did everything from clerical work to caring for orphans and acting as nurse's aides.

The remainder of the army continued to arrive from Russia. I searched the faces of the new arrivals, hoping to see the features I remembered so well, but there was still no sign of my father or Stan.

I heard many of the soldiers say that they would not have survived the trek out of Siberia without the kindness of the Russian people. Expecting nothing in return, the Russian farmers left piles of potatoes on the roadside and walked away. The Russian farmers saw our people and knew immediately what was happening. Everything the Soviets had done to us, they had already done to their own people. The Russian people suffered the consequences of Satan's system more than anyone.

It also turned out the labor camp I'd been in was not even close to being the worst. I now heard of a terrible place known as Kolyma. The men who'd been in Kolyma waited until they'd left Soviet soil to reveal their story—they were too terrified to even mention it to anyone until then. Kolyma was in northeastern Siberia, almost as far east as the Sea of Okhotsk, which is north of Japan.

"They've had camps there for years," Wolski, one of the men from Kolyma, told us one night. "There were thousands of us at the beginning."

"What kind of labor did you do?" asked Stefan.

"Gold mines," said Pingielski, also from Kolyma. "There is gold everywhere you turn."

"It's even on the ground," added Wolski. "You can walk around and pick up pieces of gold at will. It's one of the biggest secrets of the Soviet Union. The whole thing is run by the NKVD. They ship the gold to Moscow by plane. They use the gold to pay for worldwide espionage, to support Communist parties from Chicago to Shanghai, for buying influence in Western politics and Communist-friendly editorials in Western newspapers—you name it."

Walking around and picking up gold didn't seem so bad to me. "What was so bad about Kolyma?" I asked.

Pingielski leaned over to me and said very slowly, "Kolyma was a death sentence."

I looked in his eyes and believed him.

"About ten men died each day," he continued, "from starvation, or exhaustion, or both—ten a day. The temperature reached seventy degrees below zero; almost everyone lost fingers or toes."

Wolski raised his left hand. His fourth and fifth fingers were half gone. The stubs were shiny red.

"A man could last up to two years in Kolyma, no more," said Pingielski. "You were expected to work for one year, then die. They'd bring in someone to replace you, and they'd work for a year and die. It was systematic extermination."

"Twelve-hour shifts," said Wolski. "But if you didn't meet your quota, you stayed for the next shift. Fainting from weakness was considered an act of sabotage. They shot you on the spot."

"If you became an invalid from frostbite," said Pingielski, "you were taken to one of the camps for invalids. The invalids were forced to work for food like everyone else. Those without feet made baskets and chopped wood. Those without hands had to move blocks of wood with their feet."

"The non-Poles in the camp with us were mostly political prisoners," Wolski explained. "Their stories would disgrace the

Soviet Regime. Kolyma and the invalid camps are Soviet secrets; the men will never be released."

"How did you get out?" asked Stefan. "Was it the amnesty?"

"Amnesty?" Wolski chuckled humorlessly. "What amnesty? There was no amnesty in Kolyma. You work until you die, in Kolyma."

"We escaped," said Pingielski. "We didn't even hear of the amnesty until we were in Irkutsk."

"Where's that?" I asked.

"North of Mongolia," said Pingielski. "We arrived in Irkutsk and suddenly saw Poles everywhere. They told us about the amnesty. So we blended in with them and took the Trans-Siberian."

"How did you get in the army without your deportation papers?" I asked.

They both laughed. "Let's just say the army helped us out," said Wolski.

A library had been set up in the camp at General Anders' insistence, and I spent much of my free time there. I found journals and books in both Polish and English; some of them would certainly have been banned in the Soviet Union. Kaz laughed as I sat there for hours while smoking the Camel cigarettes the British so generously supplied. I started to pick up some words in English, but the reading was slow, my comprehension limited.

In school, I'd had no particular interest in history and world events were developing so rapidly in my last year in school, they were not even taught. Now, I read about the Treaty of Versailles and the rise of the Third Reich. I learned of Hitler's beer hall putsch; the formation of the sturmabtlelung, or storm troopers; the formation of the schutzstaffel, known as the SS; and the Nazi destruction of Jewish homes and shops during the "week of the broken glass."

I found out about the German annexation of the Rhineland and Czechoslovakia. Poland and Germany had worked together in 1938, when Poland seized a strip of Czech territory. But right after that, Germany applied the same pressure tactics that had destroyed Czechoslovakia against the Polish Republic.

I read about the Nazi invasion of Poland in September, 1939. The Germans came from Silesia, East Prussia, and Slovakia with 1.5 million men, or fifty-two divisions. They crossed Polish borders left unprotected at the insistence of both the French and English, so as not to provoke a war. Poland, surrounded on three sides by Germany and with only five hundred thousand Polish soldiers, couldn't defend itself against the attack.

I learned of the mutual-assistance pacts Poland had with Great Britain and France before the war, and that Chamberlain had declared in the British House of Commons, just months before, that Britain and France would lend Poland their full support if Poland were attacked. A few days after the German invasion, both England and France declared war on Germany, but didn't fire a shot.

According to the agreements Poland had made with the West, the Polish forces were expected not to defeat the Germans, but to hold them for two weeks, until the West launched their offensive; seventy French divisions were waiting near the Rhine River, ready for battle.

The Germans employed a new technique known as blitzkrieg that they'd tested during the Spanish civil war in 1938. Attacks were traditionally led by the infantry and artillery, but the German attack came on a narrow front, led by tanks and dive-bombers that split the enemy position. Wide sweeps with armored vehicles and attacks on communication followed. Rather than overpowering an enemy with brute strength, the blitzkrieg paralyzed the enemy through loss of communication and the subsequent confusion.

Air raids were launched on a number of Polish cities. Airfields, bridges, and train stations were systematically bombed. Airplanes fired machine guns into civilian refugees traveling on the roads.

The offensive from the West never came.

115

I learned about the Nazi-Soviet pact and the Soviet invasion of Poland on September seventeenth, 1939. It appeared the initiative to completely partition Poland and terminate its independent existence came from the Soviets, but the Germans quickly agreed. The Soviets played their game; they did not attack Poland simultaneously with the Germans. They waited over two weeks, to see how the West would react and to allow the Polish forces to mobilize westward toward the Germans. As the Polish forces were being defeated, the Soviets simply waltzed in from the rear. Stalin was the real winner; the Soviet Union occupied almost half of Poland with little resistance, and blocked Germany from two important objectives: Ukrainian wheat and Rumanian oil.

The information available on German-Soviet relations after the division of Poland was sketchy, but from what I could piece together, it seemed Stalin had been caught completely by surprise by the German invasion that got me out of Siberia.

Using the blitzkrieg technique and modern communications, the Germans pushed the Russians to the outskirts of Moscow. Russian communication, in contrast, was very poor—the Soviet High Command could not track a high-speed, modern war.

I discovered that blitzkrieg was used against France, which surrendered to Germany in June of 1940. The British were also under attack that year, but managed to defend their country against the German air strikes.

I started to develop an interest in military science when I found army field manuals in the library, both Polish manuals from the old army and British manuals that had been translated into Polish. When my company captain noticed my interest, he recommended reading material for me. I read about such things as the different forms of strategic offensive and defensive operations, information warfare, operational marches, military geography, and air defense operations.

Anders' Army, and my place in it, took on a whole new perspective.

The army set up a liaison office that attempted to locate family members for the soldiers. Stefan, Kaz, and I all put in requests for searches as soon as they started collecting names, but the first one to benefit was Kaz. He still did not know the whereabouts of his father, but he learned his mother and younger sister were in a British colony in Africa. They must have taken the same route we had, but our paths had never crossed. I found secret hope in this. Perhaps there was still a chance that Michal and I would be reunited with Stan, or our father.

Stefan heard nothing at all about his wife and two daughters.

Summer passed into September, and we were told we'd be departing for Iraq, no doubt to guard the oilfields.

Updates on the situation in Europe arrived as we made our preparations for departure. The Germans continued to occupy Byelorussia and the Ukraine and penetrated areas east of Moscow. There was intense fighting between the Russians and Germans in Stalingrad.

"The Germans will be finished in the winter," many of the men said. "General Frost is the best general in the Russian army—the Russian winter stops invaders every time."

When I visited Michal for the last time before our departure, I noticed his face had filled in and his lips had healed.

"This will not be like Siberia," I told him. "You will know where I am, and I'll know where you are. I'll write you, and the sisters will read my letters to you. You can write to me, too. Is it a deal?"

"Are you going to war?" he asked.

"No, nothing like that. The army is just moving, that's all."

"I'm leaving too," he said. "I'm going on a boat."

"They told you you're leaving?"

"Yeah."

"Where did they say you're going?"

"On the ocean. They said it would be fun."

I found Sister Catherine.

"Oh yes, the boat," she said. "The children went through so much on their trip from Siberia that the thought of travel scares

117

them horribly. So we prepare them for the idea of a long journey. We tell them about the fish in the sea and that, if they are lucky, we may catch some. We tell them they are very lucky—"

"But where is Michal going?"

"The government of New Zealand has agreed to take hundreds of orphans, including Michal," she said.

"New Zealand?" I repeated. She had to be joking. "Why New Zealand? It's on the other side of the world."

"Because they agreed to take him. They are a good people and they will take good care of the children."

I groped desperately for a reason why Michal shouldn't go. "But Michal isn't even an orphan," I said. "His father is alive. I know for a fact he is being held in a Soviet labor camp because he's an officer. The Russians are afraid to release the officers."

"I'm sorry, but it's better to assume a child is an orphan unless it can be verified otherwise," she said.

"I can verify it. I can produce witnesses who will tell you where they are keeping my father and the other Polish officers."

I could tell she didn't know what to say to that, and I felt a flicker of triumph. They'd let Michal stay. I'd be able to find him again, after the war.

Sister Catherine invited me to sit down with her next to a window. I tried to sit, but I couldn't stay still. *It's the sun,* I told myself; *the glare from the sun is too strong.* I stood up and turned to face her.

"I hope they release your father," she said. "But we simply do not have the facilities to accommodate all the children. We still have malnourished, sick children arriving from Russia almost every day. If we know a child has a father in the army we have tried to keep the child nearby, but we can't always do that anymore, either. Soon, the army will go off to war and all the fathers will be separated from their children. And there is also no guarantee that the war will not come here. The children and families who go to places like Africa and New Zealand will be safe."

I realized there was nothing I could do. My brother would be sent to New Zealand.

"When are they leaving?" I asked. My voice sounded flat.

"A week from tomorrow."

I went back to Michal and told him how lucky he was to be going on such a voyage. I told him I would write him as soon as I found dad and Stan. "We'll all be together again one day," I said, and forced a smile. "And you can talk to mom in your prayers." I hugged him and left.

When I returned to my tent, Kaz was laughing. He started telling me about two soldiers he'd seen get into a fight, but he noticed something was wrong and fell silent. I told him about my brother.

"You're crazy," he said. "Why are you upset? That's great news! New Zealand, Andrzej, New Zealand—beautiful green hills and valleys, fantastic lakes and beaches—New Zealand is a gem. And peace, Andrzej, peace. No Eastern Front, no labor camps, no Nazis, no Soviets. I would go there in a second, if I could."

"I don't even know if I'll ever see him again," I said.

"At least you know where he is. Look at Stefan. He hasn't found anyone from his family yet. You're lucky."

"Maybe so," I conceded. It occurred to me that I'd never thanked Sister Catherine for taking care of Michal.

# Chapter Nine

We took trucks to our destination in northern Iraq, a camp in Khanaqin that consisted of more primitive huts and an endless sea of tents pitched in the sands of the desert. The heat was sometimes unbearable, and if you didn't remember to keep drinking water, you were in danger of collapsing. The heat was actually better for Stefan's leg. His limp was less severe, and I never saw him rubbing his knee anymore.

Our army was placed under the British Tenth Army commanded by General Wilson. We took over protection of the oil fields, relieving the Eighth Indian Division. Our army underwent reconstruction that would conform it to the British model. It became a corps consisting of two infantry divisions—the Third Carpathian Infantry Division and the Fifth Kresowa Infantry—one tank brigade called the Second Armored Brigade, artillery and reconnaissance regiments, and a complement of corps units. A British liaison unit was established at General Anders' headquarters and a U.S. liaison officer was assigned to our army.

We were part of the Fifth Kresowa Infantry Division. We spent the winter training. After a series of maneuvers, we were declared ready for battle.

Stefan and I were promoted to corporal and assigned squads of eight men each. Most of the squad leaders were previous soldiers in the old army, but there weren't enough to go around, so the army was sometimes forced to elect new squad leaders, like Stefan and me.

Kaz was in my squad, as were Mikolaj, a heavyset guy from Wilno, and Boleslaw, who was only eighteen years old, a year younger than me. He hadn't been in Siberia. He'd been in the

North African Theater very briefly before being transferred into our army. Bogdan, another squad member, was from the Rzeszow area. I didn't know how he'd survived Siberia. Even after months of eating well, he looked like a toothpick. He had a narrow face and fingers so long, his hands looked like spiders. Still, he didn't look sick; quite the opposite—he always seemed to be in a good mood. He didn't seem to take anything too seriously, but he was not a weak link.

Marian, from my old squad, was transferred to an armored brigade. Jerzy, another former squad mate, was sent to General Anders' headquarters on an office assignment—the army had finally found out that he'd been a stenographer.

This excited Kaz. "Headquarters! You'll be rubbing shoulders with all the big-wigs," he told Jerzy. "When all those dignitaries throw parties, remember your old friends, and sneak us in!"

At first, I thought it might be awkward to give orders to men who were all older than me, but my age didn't bother them. I simply read the order from the lieutenant, and then made sure the order was carried out. The squad members didn't need anyone looking over their shoulders. They knew what they were doing, and we worked well as a unit.

One afternoon in late April, as my company returned to camp from a field exercise, we saw men gathered in large groups; something of importance had obviously occurred. Everyone in the camp seemed to be reading a flyer. I grabbed one from another man's hand and read:

*On the thirteenth of April 1943, Radio Berlin announced that the German Army has discovered a mass grave containing the bodies of thousands of Polish officers in the Katyn forest near Smolensk, in western Russia. The officers had been imprisoned in a camp in Kozielsk, and possibly in two other camps.*

*Based on the testimony of local inhabitants and letters and diaries found in the officers' clothing, the Germans have accused the Soviet authorities of executing the prisoners in the spring of*

*1940. The officers had their hands tied behind their backs with ropes of Russian manufacture. Tree saplings planted over the graves are now three years old.*

*After a silence of two days, the Soviet government announced that the Polish officers had been engaged in construction work near Smolensk in the summer of 1941, when the German Army overran the region and killed them.*

*The Polish government-in-exile, led by General Sikorski, has demanded an international investigation led by the International Red Cross. The Germans agreed, but the Soviet government vetoed the proposal and has broken off diplomatic relations with the Polish government in London.*

*We do not have lists of the officers' names. We will communicate further information as we receive it. We are deeply saddened by this news. However, this discovery does not change the corps' mission to free our homeland.*

*A ceremony and religious services will be conducted to honor these brave men.*

I threw the flier down and started to walk. I didn't know where I was going and I didn't care. I had some vague notion that, if I walked far or long enough, I'd leave this news, and what it meant to me, behind. I walked for several hours. As I passed the Catholic chapel, I saw a priest at the entrance, speaking to several of the soldiers—about the massacre, no doubt.

My feet carried me inside, where men were praying; I sat down. I wanted to ask God why he'd let my father die, why so many people had to die before He brought His justice to the world again. But my mind was blank; I couldn't form the prayer. I just sat there.

Eventually, I went back to my tent. Kaz was there, sprawled on his bunk, clutching a bottle of vodka. He slurred his words when he asked me if I wanted a drink, and I remembered that his father had also been an officer. I accepted the bottle he held out, and took several long swallows. I lay down. Neither of us spoke. After a while, we turned off the lights.

I was up before dawn, grateful to fall into unthinking routine. I washed and dressed and polished my boots and cleaned my gun. Then I headed to the mess tent with Kaz; we walked silently side by side.

There was much conversation in the mess hall, though.

"They told us for over a year that they let the officers out of the camps," said one man. "And now they say the Germans killed them in 1941. It's complete bullshit. The Soviets killed them alright, there's no doubt about it."

"Of course," said another. "If the Germans did it, they would have immediately accused the Soviets of the crime. Why would they wait two years?"

"If the Germans did it, why would they invite an international investigation?" asked yet another. "And if the Soviets didn't do it, why would they refuse an investigation?"

Kaz and I did not join any of the conversations. We drank some tea and then headed out for our daily assignment—an exercise in wire communications. Nobody paid much attention.

The commissioned officers were deeply affected by the discovery in the Katyn forest. The captains and lieutenants didn't bark out orders. They departed from their routine the way one departs immediately after the death of a family member. They followed protocol, but like the enlisted men, their talk turned to the massacre.

"It looks like it was the Soviets," I heard the captain tell Kaz. "And if it was the Russians, they must have some serious intentions with Poland."

As I joined them, I noticed the captain had a moustache similar to Jozef's. It looked like all the officers were imitating Anders.

"It had to be the Soviets," said Kaz. "They've been saying the officers were released for over a year."

"What intentions?" I asked.

"They wouldn't do such a thing unless they were planning something big," the captain replied.

"Like what?"

"Like establishing a permanent presence in Poland," the captain replied ominously.

Our lieutenant heard us and joined in. "Install a puppet government, you mean?"

"Exactly," said the captain. "And if that's the case, we would have to take care of the Soviets after the Germans."

"'We'?" The lieutenant shook his head. "A corps of one hundred thousand men, push out the entire Red Army? Impossible."

"It's not that simple," the captain said. "Once we were on Polish soil, our number would triple within the first hundred miles."

The idea had never occurred to me, but that was exactly what would happen. How could men not resist joining us? We were the legitimate guardians of Polish rights.

"Polish soldiers on Polish soil?" asked the captain. "How would the Soviets justify aggression to the other Allies?"

"The Germans first," cautioned the lieutenant. "A before B."

"General Frost will take care of the Germans," said the captain.

"Can we count on the Allies?" asked Kaz.

"The Allies?" The captain shrugged. "How could the Soviets justify aggression towards us? I can't see them succeeding with that. Not only with the Allies, but the whole world."

"Say what you may about the Soviets," said the lieutenant, "they have never denounced our army, and have shown no hostility towards us."

"Except for killing our officers," said Kaz.

The lieutenant gave Kaz a stare. Kaz had crossed the line between foot soldier and officer but would get away with it that day, given what had happened.

"One thing's for sure," said the captain. "The Soviets won't look on approvingly as our troops march back onto our soil and then wave good-bye as they leave for Russia."

\*\*\*

That evening, Kaz told me Jozef had approached him earlier in the day.

"He remembered that my father was an officer and he told me he was sorry to hear the news," said Kaz. "Then you know what he said? He said it's not surprising, what they did. He said the Soviets did the same thing to thousands of their own officers in the late thirties, before the war. If they did it to their own, what would stop them from doing it to us?"

I felt a little betrayed, to learn that. "You mean Jozef suspected the entire time that the Soviets killed our fathers, and never told us?"

"I guess he didn't want to upset us. Besides, he wasn't sure. We can't be sure either, Andrzej," he added.

I shook my head. I'd had enough of dashed hopes. "It would be a miracle if they survived," I said.

"Miracles happen. We got out of Siberia, didn't we? How do we know for sure that our fathers were among the dead?" asked Kaz. "We can't know for sure."

Kaz was high-strung that day. I didn't want to get into an argument with him. "I just can't see how they could have gotten out," I said.

"But you're not sure," he countered.

\*\*\*

The Catholic mass Kaz and I attended for the victims of Katyn was standing room only. A priest who had been in Siberia told us to pray for the souls of the officers who sacrificed their lives for a free and independent Poland. This was just the latest chapter in a long series of atrocities committed by totalitarian states against God-fearing people, he said. Then at the end, he said something very interesting. He said the United States and Britain made a grave error in allying themselves with the Soviet Union.

"They have made a deal with the devil," he said. "The consequences of such dealings can never be good for those true to the Lord; they can only benefit the devil.

"In Corinthians it is written: *Be ye not unequally yoked together with unbelievers: for what fellowship hath righteousness with unrighteousness? And what communion hath light with darkness? And what concord hath Christ with Belial? Or what part hath he that believeth with an infidel? And what agreement hath the temple of God with idols? For ye are the temple of the living God: as God hath said, I will dwell in them, and walk in them; and I will be their God, and they shall be my people. Wherefore come out from among them, and be ye separate, saith the Lord, and touch not the unclean thing; and I will receive you. And will be a Father unto you, and ye shall be my sons and daughters, saith the Lord Almighty."*

"What was true thousands of years ago is true now and will be forever; that is the nature of eternal truth. Britain and the United States have made a deal with one devil, hoping to defeat another devil. But little do they realize that they are dealing with the same devil. The devil has covered all corners. Even if the Soviets help the Allies defeat the Nazis, the Allies will rejoice and make concessions to the Soviets. The devil still wins, even if the Nazis lose."

He paused and took a deep breath.

"It is written: *be ye separate, saith the Lord, and touch not the unclean thing.* These brave men were massacred in a Russian forest because they remained true to the Lord. It is clearly written not to deal with the devil: *Touch not the unclean thing; and I will receive you. And will be a Father unto you, and ye shall be my sons and daughters, saith the Lord Almighty.* These men were certainly received into the Kingdom of Heaven and welcomed as sons of God."

Kaz turned to me and whispered, "Didn't the deal between Russia and Britain get us out of Siberia?"

"That's right," I said.

After the mass, Kaz approached the priest and asked him about this. The priest told him that the Germans not the British got us out of Siberia and if the Soviets had been unable to manipulate the moral weaknesses of Britain and France, we would never have been sent to Siberia in the first place.

The word was out about Soviet intentions toward Poland, and men started to pay closer attention to the latest developments, particularly on the Eastern Front. The Russians defeated the Germans in Stalingrad, but the German Army was still well into the heart of European Russia. In May, I learned General Jurgen von Arnim surrendered all Axis forces in North Africa to British and American Forces; over two hundred thousand German and Italian prisoners were taken.

\*\*\*

Bogdan fell ill with malaria. Kaz and I visited him in the infirmary occasionally. He complained of the sour tasting medicine they gave him, but his fevers passed. His was not the only case; many men were taken ill by malaria. I tried to protect myself with mosquito nets, particularly during the nights. We'd had mosquitoes in Siberia in the summer, but at least they hadn't carried malaria. That was the only good thing I could think of when it came to Siberia.

Feeling much stronger, Bogdan was in a good mood when we visited him one evening. We joked and laughed so loudly that another patient heard our laughter and entered the tent. He stood in the doorway and stared at me, but I didn't recognize him.

"Yuriy!" yelled Kaz. "It's Yuriy!" He turned excitedly toward me. "You remember, Andrzej, the Ukrainian from our camp in Siberia!"

Kaz turned back to Yuriy and waved him over. "Yuriy, we thought you were dead!"

Yuriy smiled: "Dead? No, no, not yet."

He didn't look much better than he had in the camp, except he was now clean-shaven. He took very small steps and his arms hung at his sides.

"What's wrong? Malaria?" I asked.

"Yeah, yeah, malaria." He looked for a place to sit. I pulled over a chair and he sat down slowly, bracing his hands against the arms of the chair for support.

"You must not be in our division," said Kaz. "We would have seen you by now."

"I'm with the Third Division," Yuriy said. "Are you with the Fifth?"

"That's right," I said.

"How long have you been sick?" Kaz asked.

"Oh, about a month now," Yuriy said. "At first, I didn't know what was going on. I didn't have high fevers like some of the others, but the doctor took one look at me and said it was malaria. After that, I started to spike fevers. They're gone now, though."

"When did you make it to the army?" I asked. "When did you make it to Buzuluk?"

"Oh, I wasn't in Buzuluk," he said. "The army was already in Uzbekistan when I caught up."

Here, at last, was someone who could solve the mystery of what had happened to the others from our camp. "Who came down with you?" I asked.

"Oh, there was a group of us, but no one from our barrack."

"So what happened in Siberia?" I pressed. "Did the others make it?"

"Oh, it's a long story," he said. "How about you? Did all of you make it?"

"From our group that left the valley, yes," I said. "There were a few men who disappeared during the blizzard, but the rest of us made it down to the train station."

"So what happened?" Kaz asked eagerly. "What happened after the blizzard?"

Kaz and I both leaned forward.

"Oh, I don't know," said Yuriy. "Let me think... You left at the beginning of the storm, right? Well, we all stayed in the snowbanks for the night. We did what we could to stay awake, but the next morning they found a few men frozen to death. We got scared, and about fifteen of us decided to leave. But some of the others gave us a hard time."

Kaz's voice dropped. "Kalinski?"

Yuriy paused to catch his breath. He looked at the floor and breathed through his mouth for a few seconds. "No, some of the others," he finally replied. "They said we were fools for leaving. They told us the men who froze to death hadn't stayed close to the others, like they were told to."

"Kalinski was nothing but trouble," Kaz declared. "We found out he was a general in '39. He thought he was still commanding troops."

I glanced sharply at Kaz, wondering why he hated Kalinski so much. He was exaggerating; Kalinski was not that bad.

"Kalinski, was a general?" Yuriy asked in surprise. He leaned back and looked up.

"A total nut," said Kaz. "I don't know why they all listened to him. He was obsessed with those markers."

"That wasn't even his real name," I blurted, then wondered why I was corroborating Kaz's declarations.

"No, no, it wasn't Kalinski who was telling us to stay," Yuriy protested. "Kalinski froze to death. He froze to death the first night."

Yuriy had surprised us again.

"Kalinski told everyone to stay close together," said Yuriy, "but he didn't listen to his own advice."

"So General Kalinski lost to General Frost," whispered Kaz.

"How many left with you?" I asked.

"About fifteen."

"Was Tomek with you?" I asked.

"No, I didn't see him in the morning," said Yuriy.

We sat in silence until Kaz sighed. "What happened to the rest?" he asked. "Do you know?"

"No. All I know is that twelve of us made it to Surgut. I've seen no one else. I thought you and Andrzej were dead, too." Now Yuriy leaned forward. "What about Stefan? Did he make it?"

"Yes, yes," said Kaz. "Stefan, Jozef, Patryk—they're here."

"So the others just perished?" I asked. It seemed so... unfinished.

Nobody answered. Nobody knew.

I suddenly remembered that Bogdan and Yuriy didn't know each other. I introduced them, then Yuriy glanced at me.

"How old are you now, Andrzej?" he asked.

"Twenty."

"You were just a child when you came to the camp. I couldn't believe they sent you to a prison camp. At first I thought maybe you murdered someone or something—that is, until I got to know you."

Kaz laughed. "You never know," he said. "Andrzej does look a little suspicious, now that I think about it."

Yuriy rose slowly, saying he had to lie down. We wished him well, and he left. Bogdan looked like he needed some rest as well, so Kaz and I returned to our tent.

\*\*\*

July arrived and we were moved to Palestine. By now, it was routine. The tents went down, we sat in those trucks filled with dust for hours, and then put the tents right back up in an area that looked just like the last.

Upon our arrival, I learned that Allied Forces had landed in Sicily. Mussolini had been arrested and there was a rumor that Italy was about to surrender. This made many in the corps happy, as none of us wanted to fight the Italians, who were our historic allies.

We hadn't yet been told where we would be sent, but everyone knew it would be Italy. The Germans were dug in deep in Italy, protecting a soft underbelly in the center of

Europe. An Allied invasion in Italy would force the Germans to fight a two front war, which was exactly what the Allies wanted and Germany feared.

Italy meant fighting, which both excited and terrified me. Would I survive my first battle? Would I disgrace myself? I had grown to enjoy the order of the army. Unlike Siberia, the rules were fair. But entering battle? That was another matter. My father had wanted military careers for Stan and I, but he'd never told us what it was like on the front during the Great War. Why? Were the memories too terrible to resurrect? Surely he wouldn't have wanted us to share such terror? It's the only way home, I told myself firmly. No point in worrying; I'd just have to get through it.

I was not the only one concerned. Stefan let slip that he had talked about it to Jozef, who had been on the front in '39. "Don't worry about it," Jozef said. "Siberia was worse than anything I saw on the front. If you didn't lose your mind then, it's not going to happen on the front."

Our camp in Palestine was located between Tel Aviv and Gaza, in Gedera. We spent most of our time in training and had limited contact with Palestinian Jews and Arabs, but I was stunned to find Polish spoken in every town and village. I could walk into almost any store and find someone who spoke Polish. I'd had no idea there was this little Poland in the Middle East.

While in Palestine, I learned General Sikorski, the Prime Minister and Commander-in-Chief of all Polish Armed Forces, was dead. He'd been traveling from Cairo to London when his plane crashed while landing for a stopover in Gibraltar. Men just shook their heads when they heard the news. We thought the death was very suspicious, as there'd recently been two attempts on his life. The year before, a bomb was found on a plane he was to take to the United States. Not long after that, a plane he was to take from Scotland to London was sabotaged. Most said the Soviets were behind it—more evidence of their plans to dominate a postwar Poland.

One Friday evening, Kaz got a pass to go into Tel Aviv. He planned to buy gold coins. As he put on his clean uniform, he explained profit margins to me.

"You can triple your money, easy," he told me. "Gold is three or four times more expensive in Italy, and I hear it is easy to sell."

"I'm not looking to make a profit," I said. "I just want to get out alive."

"So you get out broke, and then what?"

"My father told me he saw more men die of greed than anything else in the Great War."

"That was different. It was a different war," Kaz said as he buttoned his pressed shirt. "Besides, I'm not looking to steal the Mona Lisa. It's just a few coins. There is no harm to anyone. The people here want to sell and in Italy, they want to buy. I'm only providing a service." He started to comb his hair, then paused. "What did he mean by that, anyway?"

"My father?"

"Yeah. Men were killing each other over loot?"

"No, I think he meant they took unnecessary chances," I said.

"What army was he in?" asked Kaz.

"The Polish Legions, but I don't think he meant that's where the looting was. He just said there was a lot of looting and greed during the war. Anyway, I'm not interested in the coins," I added.

"Suit yourself."

The next morning in the mess hall, I asked Stefan about the gold coins. He put a greasy sausage back down on his plate and waved his arms for emphasis as he said, "Forget it. It's nothing but trouble. It won't make you rich, and you can get into trouble. What if they expelled you from the army? What would you do? Where would you go? Forget it. Have some breakfast."

I still relied on Stefan's judgment as much as I had when I was seventeen years old. He had yet to steer me wrong.

\*\*\*

In November we were moved to Egypt, no doubt our last stop before being sent to Italy. It came as no surprise to us to learn that General Anders was meeting with General Henry Wilson, who was the Allied commander in Italy. Although most of the soldiers in our corps were those who had escaped Siberia, the Allies now transferred other Polish soldiers into the corps, including men who had fought in North Africa.

One afternoon in late November, I received my first piece of mail. The postmark read Wellington, N.Z.—Michal! He'd gotten there safely! I excitedly ripped open the envelope.

The letter was written in a child's own hand—Michal's; I had forgotten he was already eight years old. My smile grew as I read; for the first time, I felt a sense of normalcy, a sense of some order in my life similar to the order of the army, only this was personal.

The letter was a tumble of boyish observations: He wrote that the trip on the sea was much longer than he thought it would be, that the boys spent their time on the ship watching soldiers practice shooting their guns, and that he now lived at the Polish Children's Camp in Pahiatua. His best friend's name was Olek, and Olek's bed was right next to his. The boys played a game with a stick and a ball called cricket. Michal couldn't join the team; they said he was too young, but they did let him practice. They sang Polish songs and danced, but Michal didn't like that part. He liked it when they had a campfire. He ended the letter by asking me if I had found dad and Stan.

I stared at the letter. Where was Stan; where was my older brother? I felt like shouting it: "Damn you Stan, where are you?" In that sense, I was still powerless. I could not look for Stan. He would either show up eventually, or he wouldn't. There was nothing I could do to change that.

When I wrote Michal back, I described our travels in the army. *I am still looking for dad and Stan,* I wrote. I wished him

Robert Ambros

well and reminded him that he could always talk to mom in his prayers. As I addressed the envelope, I paused. I still could not get over these people in New Zealand. They took orphans from another continent that didn't even speak their language and gave them the environment they needed. After living through Siberia, it seemed almost like a miracle to me that such people existed.

Kaz, meanwhile, could not get over a comedian named Lou Costello. The British sent us movies every Friday, and many featured the little fat guy. "He's a genius," said Kaz. "Look at those gestures, the hand movements—it's fantastic."

Kaz was not the only fan; the movies featuring Costello were a favorite among the men, though I liked the serious movies that starred the American actor, Bogart.

"Look at that guy," whispered Bogdan during a showing. "He's a plumber and he has a car like that."

"It's the movies," said Stefan. "They can show you whatever they want to. It's not real."

Someone yelled for us to shut up.

"If it's a fake, just for show, how could they pass it off as real to their own people?" countered Bogdan.

"Shut up," we heard from the rear.

"It's the movies," repeated Stefan.

"Must be some truth to it," Bogdan mused. "Now *that's* the place to live."

I had to agree with Bogdan. We couldn't just dismiss what these movies showed us. There must have been some truth to it.

"Fix some pipes and buy a Ford," said Bogdan. "That's for me."

***

In December we finally got the word: the corps would be deployed to Italy in waves. My company was given orders to deploy in late January. We took trucks to Alexandria and boarded ships bound for Italy. Bogdan remarked that this was the first time we were moving north as an army.

"Our first step home," Kaz said.

We landed in Taranto, a port on the southern tip of Italy. It felt strange to step onto European soil with a rifle on my back. As we made our way north, we learned what was happening from the soldiers who'd arrived before us.

"The Allies want Rome badly, and they want it now," I heard. To capture one of the three capitals of the Axis—Berlin, Rome, and Tokyo—would be of great psychological importance to the Allies.

Italy had in fact surrendered, and German troops marched into Rome and took control of the capital. The Allied campaign in Italy began that summer, but there had been little progress; the situation deteriorated into a near stalemate.

They told us Field Marshall Kesselring, one of Hitler's top defensive strategists, commanded the Germans in Italy. The mountainous terrain of Italy's boot, with its poor roads and many rivers, tremendously favored the defender. The German engineers had built a number of fortified lines. They were well positioned in the hills, and shelled Allied positions at will.

"Modern weapons are useless," they said.

Kesselring was defending what was called the Gustav Line, which ran south of Rome from the Tyrrhenian to the Adriatic Sea. The Allies tried to bypass the line by landing fifty thousand American troops in Anzio. They caught the Germans by surprise and met with little initial resistance, but now the Germans were staging a counteroffensive.

I asked one of the soldiers if anyone had any news from the Eastern Front.

"The Russians have launched a winter offensive and are pushing the Germans back into Byelorussia," he said. But that was not news to us; we had heard that a month ago.

We made our way north in trucks and camped for the night. Rations were distributed, but my stomach was in knots and I couldn't eat. Tomorrow, I would have to put everything I'd learned into practice. What if I forgot?

I lit a Camel and forced myself to think back to the manuals I'd read on mountain fighting, trying to commit everything to memory as though studying for an exam. But failing this exam would be fatal. I shook that thought out of my head, stubbed out the Camel, and closed my eyes in concentration.

*Campaigns in mountains consist of a series of separate battles,* I recalled. *Operations are focused on smaller units: platoons and companies. The defender has the obvious advantage. The attacker must focus on deception, surprise actions, and attaining key terrain. Lead elements secure the high ground and provide cover for the rest. Surprise attacks can be very successful in mountainous terrain. Use rough, unlikely routes and periods of poor visibility to avoid detection.*

I paused and mentally repeated that. It seemed more applicable to my personal survival than talk of troop movements in general.

*Plan movements to coincide with other operations. Use of tanks and armored vehicles is limited to the valleys. Mobilize for attack when visibility is poor; slow movement in poor visibility actually decreases the enemy's ability to sense what is happening. The enemy will defend against an attacker in the valley with flanking fires and artillery. All terrain features that can be taken by a small enemy force must be secured. Do not halt on a ridgeline during an attack, which the enemy can target...* Ah, something else that bore repeating.

*When the enemy is well hidden, attack by encirclement is not favored, due to the possibility of enemy flank defense; attack across a broad front along multiple axes is preferable.*

That was all I could remember. For a moment I felt a surge of panic; how would I remember everything? I reminded myself that I would not have to make these decisions. All I had to do was get the order from the lieutenant and issue it to all the members of my squad.

Kaz approached me with a tin can in one hand and a fork in the other: "Hey, you know what I just heard one guy say?" he asked.

"I can't eat," I blurted. "It's my stomach."

He paused with his mouth open and looked at me a moment, then dismissed my announcement and continued. "He said 'from Italy to our Polish land.' You know, like in the national anthem."

"Where does that come from, anyway?" I asked, welcoming conversation—anything that would take my mind off tomorrow.

Kaz frowned, but I could tell by his eyes that he'd decided to take a shot at me. "What kind of school did you go to, anyway?"

"It was a good school," I said, smiling. "I just wasn't interested in history."

"It's from when they partitioned Poland in the eighteenth century. Napoleon agreed to create Polish legions in Italy. They were émigrés and prisoners of war, like us. General Dombrowski led them, you know, to regain Polish land. You know the phrase from the anthem: 'March, march Dombrowski! From Italy to our Polish land, let us now unite the nation under your command.'"

We were tired from the trip but when the men nearby started comparing what we were doing to the words from our national anthem, our excitement grew. This was the closest we had been to Poland in a long time. The northern border of Italy was only three hundred miles from southern Poland. From where we were, it was probably eight hundred miles away. After what we had been through, eight hundred miles was nothing. Our homes were not far away, and everyone could feel it.

\*\*\*

We were given our first assignment the next day: patrol land running along the Sangro River. The area was quite a ways east of the front; the idea must have been to prevent the Germans from outflanking the Allies.

As we moved to the area in trucks, we encountered divisions from other armies for the first time. We passed the Indian Eighth Infantry Division, the same division we had replaced in

Iraq. They wore the same British uniforms we did. We waved to each other and smiled, which was all we could have done. Even if we stopped, we didn't speak each other's language.

War had devastated the Italian countryside and the villages we passed through. Bombs had left crumbling shells where buildings had once stood, and raw craters in the ground. The people appeared starved. Many of the children begged Allied soldiers for food.

"What's that 'T' on their shoulders?" someone asked as we passed a battalion of American soldiers.

Nobody seemed to know what the patch on the Americans' uniforms stood for.

"It stands for Texas," a lieutenant finally replied. "They're the Thirty-sixth Texas Division."

"Cowboys!" someone yelled, and men laughed.

Now I've seen everything, I thought, cowboys from Texas with a gripe against Hitler—we're not the only ones who've come a long way.

We reached the Sangro River in a cold rain. My stomach tightened again; it occurred to me that what might start as a routine defensive patrol could quickly turn into a full-scale battle. But the patrol turned out to be uneventful. We patrolled the region for weeks, all the while trying to get information on the fronts. I watched the situation in Italy with one eye and the Eastern Front with the other. I heard the Eastern Front line was moving closer to Poland, but I had no specific information.

One evening, Stefan ran into our tent and announced that General Anders had spoken to the people in occupied Poland via a BBC radio broadcast, two nights past.

"To those in Poland?" Kaz repeated, skeptical. The Germans declared such transmissions illegal, and anyone caught listening to them risked being shot by the Germans.

I didn't understand why Stefan found the news so exciting. "What does that have to do with us?" I asked.

Stefan grinned. "Because among other things, he was talking about us—his army. Look, our friend Jerzy lent me a copy of the transcript."

"A transcript of a radio speech?" Kaz exclaimed as Stefan pulled some papers from his breast pocket and unfolded them. "Who wants a copy of a radio speech? He was supposed to sneak us into fancy dinner parties."

Stefan ignored him and flattened the papers out on his leg, then stepped over to the light to read them.

"I don't want a transcript," Kaz protested. "I want champagne and smoked salmon. I want to chat with a lonely Jean Harlow, who misses America terribly." But he stepped up to read over Stefan's shoulder with me.

"Be quiet, Kaz," I muttered, craning to see the words on the paper.

Stefan glanced over his shoulder, then held the papers up higher. "There, can you see?" he asked. "Jerzy knew you'd be interested; what with all the reading you've been doing."

Smiling, I nodded, then read:

*We are proud of the glory with which Polish soldiers covered themselves when, in 1939, they fought against overwhelming odds and when, at the most crucial moment, they were treacherously stabbed in the back. We are proud of our airmen and our sailors, who as allies of Great Britain fought in defense of the British Isles in the critical days of 1940. We are proud of the magnificent steadfastness of our soldiers, whose gallantry has been acknowledged by the whole world, on the fields of France, in the fjords of Norway, and on the sands of the African desert. But it is with the greatest pride and gratitude that we look up to you, the people of Poland, who have never lost your faith, and for so many years have continued to fight in defense of Poland.*

*From the moment when our troops find themselves on the old historic road, when the Germans feel the might of our arms, I want to assure you that we shall do our duty as soldiers fighting for the independence of Poland. Amongst us are soldiers from Tobruk and Gazala, soldiers from Narvik and from the fields of France, and the great majority have been through prisons and concentration camps in the far north. We went through wild and deserted spaces and were decimated by frost, epidemics and our enemies.*

*We now follow the ancient road of the Dombrowski legions. We have experienced much already, and still we have to face much bitterness on our way. We shall fight the Germans without respite because we all know that without defeating Germany, there will be no Poland.*

*We cannot accept even in our thoughts that any of our enemies will be able to take away even a small part of Polish land.*

*We trust that our great Allies and friends—Great Britain and the United States—whose armies are fighting shoulder to shoulder with us, will assist us to make Poland rise again free and independent, truly strong and great, securing happiness for the now bleeding Polish nation.*

*Over mountains, rivers, and forests let our soldierly song reach you: Poland is not yet lost.*

\*\*\*

The Germans were positioned in the mountains south of Rome, and the Allies had been unable to break through. There was only one pass through the range and the Gustav line: the Liri River valley. But the valley was blocked by several hills, the key hill being Monte Cassino. A town of the same name lay at its base, and a medieval Benedictine monastery perched on its top. The Germans had not disturbed the monastery, but fortified themselves well on the hill with barbed wire, mines, concrete bunkers, and machine gun nests. Attackers from any quarter were subjected to strong crossfire from both artillery and firearms. The position was considered impregnable.

The Allies had tried to take Cassino several times; in January, General Mark Clark had commanded the American Fifth Army in the first attempt, which included the Second and Tenth American Army Corps, the French Expeditionary Corps, and the British X Corps.

The Texas division, the Thirty-sixth—the soldiers with the 'T' on their shoulder patches that we'd seen during our transport—tried to take it first. They approached from the valley on a narrow front and met with heavy casualties. The French Expeditionary Corps attacked on the right wing, trying unsuccessfully to outflank Monte Cassino from the north. The British X Corps' attack on the southern flank of the Gustav line also failed.

Next, the Thirty-fourth U.S. Infantry Division was ordered to attack the town of Monte Cassino and capture hills to its north. The Americans actually made it to the top if the hill, but were pushed back by a parachute division and suffered heavy losses again.

The Second New Zealand and the Fourth Indian Divisions were then called in. Both these divisions were famous for their achievements in Africa. During this attempt, hundreds of bombers attacked the monastery from the air and completely destroyed it, which only helped the Germans. The remains of the monastery's walls and cellars were fortified and used in the Germans' defense. Worse, the Allied ground forces had not been told about the bombing, so the bombing was not followed by an immediate ground attack. The Germans had a chance to regroup.

The New Zealand and Indian Corps launched a second attack, but they, too, suffered heavy casualties and withdrew. Another aerial bombardment preceded a third ground assault, which made some progress before a German counterattack forced our troops to withdraw.

Kaz burst into our tent one morning in April and announced, "We've got Monte Cassino." He waited, almost bouncing up and down on the balls of his feet, while I finished toweling off my face and then stared at him.

"Monte Cassino? The Americans have been slaughtered there."

"Well, a sector adjacent to Monte Cassino, but you know what it means. The British want to find out how serious we are about fighting."

Men were anxious to fight, but the British wondered how effective and committed to battle a man could be when, just eighteen months ago, he'd been emaciated and half-starved. Monte Cassino would certainly show our mettle, I thought.

In early May, we learned of General Anders' plan for Monte Cassino. The key to the German defense had been their ability to shift from sector to sector and successfully counterattack any offensive. His plan was to capture a number of key hills simultaneously, thereby preventing the Germans from coordinating their fire, and forcing them to disperse their reserves.

The Germans had no idea that a Polish Army was here and that was the way General Anders wanted to keep it. No patrols were sent out to reconnoiter the enemy positions. All movement would be at night.

Stefan voiced what we all thought: "They'll be stunned to learn who we are," he said of the Germans. "They'll be facing an enemy again that they thought they'd already beaten."

We received our battalion orders and an order from General Anders himself that read:

*Soldiers!*

*The moment for battle has arrived. We have long awaited the moment for revenge and retribution over our ancient enemy. Shoulder to shoulder with us will fight British, American, Canadian, and New Zealand divisions, together with the French, Italian, and Indian troops.*

*The task assigned to us will cover the glory the name of the Polish soldier all over the world.*

*At this moment the thoughts and the hearts of our whole nation will be with us.*

*Trusting in the Justice of Divine Providence we go forward with the sacred slogan in our hearts: God, Honor, Country.*

*Wladyslaw Anders, Lt-General*
*Commander, II Polish Army Corps*

I understood exactly what General Anders referred to. Not only would a victory here give courage to the underground resistance movement in Poland, but a Polish victory in Cassino would open up the road to Rome and make headlines throughout the world. The entire world watched and waited for the liberation of Rome. The entire world would see how serious we were in fighting for a free Poland. And, to those Poles dispersed around the globe by war, hearing that Poles were back in the war and winning battles against Nazis would do much for their morale.

# Chapter Ten

I remembered what Jozef once told me, that men would climb a mountain for Anders. Well, there I was climbing a mountain, but I never thought I would have to climb the same mountain over and over again. If I had not been so tired, I would have found the idea humorous.

Ammunition, food, water, gasoline, and engineering equipment were brought up, first by truck, then by jeep on the narrowest trails, and then up the slopes by foot or donkey. Although we were part of a rifle company, my squad helped an artillery unit transport large guns up the slope. The pieces were disassembled at the base and reassembled once into position on the upper slope.

We did all of this at night. Any move in the daylight would have drawn German fire. We spent the daylight hours in makeshift camouflaged shelters. On nights with a bright moon, we used smoke screens to hide our movements.

I was surprised to see the level of determination in the men, particularly the soldiers of '39. They shifted into high gear and worked with tremendous resolve.

As we prepared our positions, the engineers widened mountain tracks into roads wide enough for tanks to pass. In some cases, they created roads from scratch. They worked feverishly at night and stopped all activity at daybreak. To allow artillery units to fire, trees were cut down, but they were held upright by wire so their absence wouldn't draw any suspicion from the enemy.

As we prepared for the attack, everyone forgot about mealtimes. I could have made trips up and down the hill all night and not known where the nearest rations were stored. I carried over two pounds of chocolate with me up and down the mountain and never considered eating it. I wouldn't eat it, unless I could not find food anywhere and I was very hungry.

Siberia had made us different from others; it was second nature for us to eat a meal and slip the bread skins into our pockets. We hadn't worried about food since reaching Iran, but every so often, I found my pockets stuffed with bread skins, and tossed them. We knew it was irrational to store food in this manner—even embarrassing, when one of the soldiers who hadn't been in Siberia saw us do it—but those of us who'd been in Siberia understood.

On May eleventh, General Sulik, the commander of our division, ordered our battalion to clear Phantom Ridge and secure the Colle San Angelo Ridge, two of the key points to be taken simultaneously.

As darkness fell, the trees suddenly came down and the air reverberated with the pounding of artillery. Shells rained down on the German infantry. For a full hour, their thunder filled the valleys.

*This is it,* I thought as I waited with my squad for the order to move. Around me, white flashed in the dusk—the whites of my squad members' eyes, their teeth as they breathed through parted lips. Did I look like that? I adjusted my grip on my rifle, then wiped first one sweaty palm, then the other on my pant legs. As I reached to make sure Michal's letter was still in my chest pocket, I noticed that my hand trembled.

At 0100 hours we attacked. *Just like the exercises,* I told myself as I led my squad down the hill in wedge formation. I was breathing so hard, I could barely hear the shells exploding. Cover, fire, and move, I repeated to myself over and over. It took a moment for the rat-tat of machine gun fire to register in my consciousness. To our front and on the flanks, a detached part of my brain noted.

Everything went white in a split-second flash that burned into my retinas. *God, please let me get through this!* I prayed as another flash, then another lit up the terrain as if it were noon. The Germans were using illuminating shells to uncover us.

My breathing was a harsh, sawing rasp but I kept going, imitating the veteran soldiers from the army of '39. They moved aggressively through the firestorm, and my feet followed them seemingly of their own volition. My squad followed me.

Heavy machine gun fire ripped across our path from a high point on our right. The veteran soldiers quickly sought cover, and I did the same. "MG42s," a veteran sprawled in the scrub next to me muttered. He kept his eyes on the cave where a strobe-like flash gave away their location as the machine guns fired. MG42s were so fast, the gunners fired in short spurts instead of continuously. They could concentrate on accuracy.

Now all movement slowed, almost came to a standstill. We crouched behind rocks and fallen trees. Grenades arced into the cave. A tremendous explosion roared from the cave and shuddered the ground beneath me. We scuttled forward, took cover, took out another nest, and scrambled forward again. I started to get a feel for it—slow, slow, slow, then fast, fast, fast. We'd had exercises on movement, but real battle had its own tempo. Once I got used to the pattern, I fell back on my training and trusted that and luck to keep me alive.

It took several hours to reach the foot of Phantom Ridge. As we approached, a smell that had registered only subliminally on my overloaded senses grew to an unpleasant, cloying odor, then a stench that made me gag. It overpowered everything—the smoke, the smell of gunpowder, the delicate, misplaced green smell from the poppies we crushed under our boots.

Distracted by the smell, I wasn't concentrating on my footing on the uneven terrain. A tree trunk, lost in the sea of poppies, hooked my boot and I went down. I instinctively threw my hands, still gripping my rifle, forward to break my fall. The rifle struck the buried tree trunk, held a moment, then slowly sank lower—and the reek of rotten meat slammed into me. It sent me scrambling backward, crablike.

Bile churned up my throat. As I leaned over to release it, I caught sight of the source of the terrible odor. The decaying body of a man—bloated, mottled, its face more skull than flesh—lay sprawled as he'd fallen and died, amidst the poppies.

Desperately wiping my hands on the trampled grass on either side of me, I looked around. Bodies lay everywhere. Some wore German helmets; others bore the Texan 'T' patch on their shoulders. We were in no man's land. The battle here had been going on for months, and neither side had been able to remove its dead.

I rose and pushed forward. I could not find our lieutenant at the foot of the hill. A lieutenant from the platoon to our right told my squad to follow him. We started up the ridge.

Heavy fire suddenly burst from the left flank, splitting our company in two. I saw the platoons on our left retreating, only to be stopped by machine gun fire from the rear.

"How the hell did they get behind us?" someone yelled.

"Check behind us," the lieutenant told me. "See what's going on."

I crawled up to a boulder and peered around it, but couldn't see anything. A thick patch of woods lay just twenty feet ahead of me. I leaped to my feet and ran for all I was worth, high-stepping desperately over the enemy bullets that shot across my path.

Once in the woods, I crawled up to a high point and finally saw where the fire was coming from—a point we'd passed just minutes ago. The nest had been covered by bushes then, but now I saw a machine gun squad in the opening of what looked like a small cave. A platoon of our men was trapped in a patch of woods between one machine gun squad to their left rear and another dead ahead of them.

"It's just a squad," I yelled back to the lieutenant. "It's just a squad in a cave." I waited until I heard some of our fire and crossed the open space back to my platoon.

"We'll advance," the lieutenant told us, but before we moved, someone ran up to him.

"Pull back!" he yelled. I recognized Jozef; he had a platoon of men with him. I felt safer, knowing Jozef was near. "Pull back and take out that cave, or those men are dead," he told the lieutenant.

"But the orders—"

"These are your new orders," Jozef yelled. "Pull back, take out those MG42s in the cave, and hold your position. There's no point in trying to make it to the top now. We made it up, but had to withdraw."

The lieutenant signaled for the men to pull back. Suddenly, shells slammed into us from the front. Everyone fell to the ground.

I lay there with my cheek pressed to the ground and my eyes closed, feeling the shower of dirt the shells had displaced raining onto my back and helmet and legs. I drew breath, choked in the thick smoke, and wheezed and coughed for several minutes.

In the relative stillness after the shelling stopped, I heard moaning. I cracked my eyelids open and made out a figure lying on the ground about twenty feet ahead of me. Jozef!

I jumped to my feet and ran over to him, then stopped, staring in horror at my friend. His right leg was blown off. The right side of his abdominal wall was gone. His intestines spilled out over the ground. My throat closed; I fell to my knees beside him. I didn't know what to do. I stared at his guts and then at his face.

His breathing was heavy. I don't know if he even saw me; his eyes stared up into the air.

"Medics!" I yelled. "Medics!"

He suddenly cried out and tried to lift his body by putting his weight on his left arm. He managed to flop onto his left side. He started hitting the ground with his right fist, pounding the earth with all his might. I stared in numb horror as his fist slammed again and again against the ground, narrowly missing the shiny coils of his intestine.

The blows grew weaker. I leaned forward and took over for him. I pounded the earth as hard as I could. I didn't know why.

I just pounded harder and harder, right in the spot he had been pounding. Tears stung my eyes. I smashed and smashed the poppies until their red petals were indistinguishable from the blood pooled around them. Jozef's blood.

Medics finally arrived. They put a tourniquet around what was left of his right leg and then injected something into his left leg. They injected him over and over and finally his head fell back and he slumped on the ground. His breathing became shallow and he turned white. The two medics stood over him, frowning. They shook their heads, as if someone had asked them if they wanted to bet on a soccer team and they'd just decided against it.

I looked back down at Jozef and caressed his forehead with my hand. He looked at me but his eyes seemed to look right past me. His breathing grew more and more shallow, until it stopped altogether. I stayed beside him.

I heard grenades, then men yelling that the MG42s were taken out. The medics came back, walking slowly. They glanced at me but didn't say anything as each gripped Jozef's collar and dragged his body away.

I knelt alone in a field of poppies and dead men. After a moment I rose, looked around, and numbly returned to the living.

The men were digging out fighting positions, preparing to hold ground. Some dug; others aligned the trunks of dead trees. No one talked. I could hear shelling in the adjacent hills. The shelling stopped just before sunrise, then resumed suddenly on our side of the hill as the Germans started a daylight counteroffensive.

We'd practiced building firing positions for months and it paid off now—we were dug in well. We held our position as the Germans charged. The German's counterattack failed.

An order came to retreat. We pulled back our wounded. Eighteen-year-old Boleslaw of my squad was hurt, hit in the leg. He couldn't walk, so I and one of the medics dragged him back with us.

We were ordered back to our starting point, where the medics cared for the wounded and the others rested. I sat down and tried to think of something—anything—I should do. Rations. I had to check rations. And equipment. It came back to me: as squad leader, I had to inspect the squad; check the rations, water, weapons, ammunition, and equipment. I then had to report to the lieutenant.

I encountered Stefan on my way to report.

"Why did they call us back?" he asked. "We had the position."

"I don't know," I said as he offered me a Camel and I took it.

"How's your squad?" he asked.

"Jozef's dead," I said.

Stefan didn't react at all.

We sat down together and smoked in silence. I felt myself swaying with exhaustion.

Bogdan joined us. "The captain said they called us back because we couldn't take either Phantom Ridge or San Angelo. The Third division took both Hill 593 and Hill 569, but couldn't hold them because of us."

He paused, listening, then asked, "Do you hear those loudspeakers?" He had a smile on his face. Someone seemed to have forgotten to tell Bogdan this was real war. "You won't believe what the Germans are saying. They discovered we're Poles, and now they're trying to persuade us to join the German side. They are offering us a free Poland in return."

Stefan chuckled. I just shook my head. What a bizarre invitation! It revealed how little they knew of their enemy. We'd crossed Siberia with rags on our feet to get here, and survived extreme hardship. Did they think we didn't know they'd invaded Poland?

Our platoon leader had not survived the battle. His replacement approached us and took our report on dead, wounded, rations, and ammunition.

"How is Boleslaw?" I asked him.

He chuckled. It turned out Boleslaw was more terrified than injured. He had a flesh wound in the thigh, but the medics had stopped the bleeding. The lieutenant told us to await orders.

"When will we go again?" I asked.

"We're waiting to hear the progress of the British Thirteen Corps," he said.

"How did we do?" asked Stefan.

"We lost twenty percent of the soldiers in our division," he admitted, then added, "but the Germans were hurt much worse."

The entire day passed without new orders. We received our rations and ammunition and then bedded down for the night.

When I went to see Boleslaw in the morning, the medics told me he was dead. I just stared at them, stunned. "Yesterday you told me you'd stopped the bleeding and Boleslaw would be fine," I protested. "Now you tell me he's dead?" They only shrugged. I had no idea what had happened.

The new order came the next day. A fresh battalion was replacing us; we could continue to rest.

The shelling began as in the first attack. The new battalions headed for the same targets we had. This time, our tanks made it onto the slopes of Phantom Ridge and provided covering fire for the infantry as they took Phantom Ridge.

It turned out our rest period was not very long. We were sent back in to take San Angelo under the command of an armored regiment. If we took San Angelo, another key point, Massa Albaneta, could be seized.

As we regrouped at the foot of San Angelo prior to our assault, Kaz ran up to me and yelled, "Those are cooks!"

"What do you mean?" I asked, glancing and looked to Kaz for an explanation.

"Look at those guys, they're cooks," he said, and pointed. "Look, it's Gabielski."

Sure enough, further down the line, there was our company cook, Gabielski, holding a rifle. It appeared Anders had ordered everyone to the front line, even cooks and drivers.

"He's risking it all on this battle," said Kaz.

*Seeing a cook with a rifle in his hands should probably scare the hell out of me,* I thought—it would normally be a sign of desperation. Instead, the sight gave me a strange rush. To me, it signaled determination, a total commitment to victory. *Jozef,* I thought, *they're going in for the kill.*

The fight for San Angelo went on. The order came to attack, and we scrambled up the slope amidst the smoke and screams and thunder of battle, slipping on the churned earth and who knew what else. I had an idea what to expect this time, but my mouth went dry and my heart pounded against my ribs, just as it had the day before-or perhaps *because* I knew what to expect this time.

Machine gun fire ripped narrow trenches in the trampled grass and vegetation around us and sent sheets of dirt into the air. I saw men ahead of me blown to bits as they triggered German trip lines that ran from concealed pillboxes to grenades concealed in the grass. Bodies amidst the poppies faded in comparison to what lay hidden here.

Someone ahead signaled and I dropped to the ground with those around me, senses in overdrive as I listened, looked, for the threat. I saw a German pillbox a short ways up the slope. I waited for the rat-tat of machine gun fire and the telltale flash from the pillbox's narrow firing aperture, but none came. After a moment, someone hollered back that it was clear, and I rose and joined a group of soldiers peering inside the pillbox.

The air inside was thick with the iron tang of blood. Four dead Germans lay in dark pools of their own blood. Each had been stabbed several times. Blood splattered the walls. None of the Germans had drawn their handguns or lifted a rifle. The attack must have been quick and vicious.

"Who would attack a pillbox with knives?" the man beside me asked, staring at the slashed bodies.

"The soldiers from the old army," I supplied, suddenly realizing what must have happened. "The same men who were defeated by the Germans in '39. They must have run out of ammunition." Men who had spent two years in Soviet labor camps, thinking about those battles, would have no reservations about using knives.

We continued our advance, passing dead and wounded in our ascent. But there were more dead Germans than our own— many more.

We took the peak, but ran out of ammunition. The Germans launched a counterattack, and we hunkered down, preparing to repel it as best we could.

Crouched in my foxhole, I caught glimpses of German soldiers as they crept towards us, and wondered how I would do up close, with a knife. The soldiers of '39 had a sense of revenge to fuel their blows; I'd suffered more at the hands of Russians than those of Germans.

I ducked back into my hole and pressed my body against its earthen wall as the ground erupted a short distance in front of my position. *I may not have to worry about knives,* I thought, breathing the rich, moist smell of the dirt I'd pressed my face against; *I may just get blown to pieces by a grenade or sliced up by shrapnel.*

I heard a ragged cheer as our division's Commando Company arrived. Under their fire, the enemy retreated. Relief unwound my tense muscles as I sheathed my knife. Our mission was complete. All we had to do now was hold our position and see if the other battalions reached their goals. Exhausted, I sat in my foxhole and watched the pall of smoke that gradually rose from the valleys. When it reached us, it stung our eyes and burned our throats. But we could finally rest.

Dusk came, accompanied by intensive shelling on the neighboring hills. The artillery eventually stopped, and the night became quiet. At this time of year, we should have heard birdsong, even insects. But the only sounds we heard were the moans of the dying and the caw of the crows feeding on them. Isolated rifle shots echoed sporadically through the hills.

In the morning, I learned it was over. The Germans had retreated during the night, leaving only some of their wounded behind.

Someone told me that the Twelfth Lancers Regiment planted a Polish flag atop the ruin of the monastery on Monastery Hill. The regiment couldn't find a Polish flag, the tale went, so they cut the red material out of a Red Cross flag and sewed together white handkerchiefs collected from the men to make a red and white Polish flag. When General Anders came by, he told the men to plant a Union Jack, as well. I would have liked to have seen it, but we received the order to head out.

We packed up our things and headed out to Piedimonte, a town built of stone overlooking the Liri Valley. Piedimonte commanded a natural defensive position over the main road running through the valley, and the Germans had fortified this stronghold well, reinforcing their machine gun nests and artillery positions with concrete. When we reached the area, we found out that this was to be mainly a tank operation, and we'd be held in reserve. I noticed that Sherman tanks had replaced many of the older tanks our armored units had trained with.

The battle for Piedimonte lasted for five days. Piedimonte exhausted me, even though I was in reserve. The fighting went on day and night; the constant flashes and thunder of artillery fire made sleeping impossible. When Piedimonte was finally taken, the Thirteenth British Army Corps was able to progress up the valley without interference.

Around this time, the statistics from Cassino were announced, and I realized that my first battle had been horrific, and not just because it was my first: almost nine hundred killed, three thousand wounded, and over 100 missing, before the Germans sensed they were being surrounded and decided to retreat.

After Piedimonte, our high officers congratulated us and granted a few days' R&R before sending us on our next assignment, somewhere on the Adriatic Coast.

The British had no more doubts about our willingness to fight. In fact, they appeared very impressed with our performance, and placed some of their own troops under the command of the Polish Corps, including two British artillery regiments, armored cavalry, and several battalions of the Italian Corps.

One day, General Sir Harold Alexander, Commander-in-Chief of the Allied Armies in Italy, paid us a visit. All our battalions were represented, as was a platoon of armored vehicles from the British Eighth Army.

During a ceremony held in a clearing in the woods near Monte Cassino, General Alexander said, "In the name of His Majesty George VI, King of Great Britain, I confer on you the Order of the Bath," as he decorated General Anders with a high reward for military service that had originated in the medieval knighthoods.

He then turned and addressed the assembled battalions: *By conferring on General Anders the Order of the Bath, my Sovereign has decorated the Commander of the II Army Corps for his excellent leadership, and also by it expressed his appreciation for the extreme gallantry and great spirit of self-sacrifice shown by the Polish soldiers during the battle of Monte Cassino. It was a day of great glory for Poland, when you took this stronghold the Germans themselves considered to be impregnable. It was the first stage of a major battle that you went through for the European fortress. It is not merely a brilliant beginning: it is a signpost showing the way to the future. Today I can sincerely and frankly tell you that.*

*Soldiers of the II Polish Corps, if it had been given to me to choose the soldiers I would like to command, I would have chosen the Poles. I pay my tribute to you.*

\*\*\*

We finally had a chance to relax. Despite the casualties, morale was high; we had proven ourselves in battle and we allowed ourselves the luxury of thinking about home. The Germans were north, and that was where our homes were. We were committed to continue pushing them north until we were in Poland. We would push them into the Baltic Sea if we had to, we thought. We had a long way to go, but we were the ones who opened up the road to Rome, something the Allies had been trying unsuccessfully to do for months.

Time to relax meant time for talk, and during one conversation, I learned something quite unexpected. When Germany invaded Poland in 1939, they forced hundreds of thousands of young Polish men into the German Army. When we captured German soldiers, our corps found Poles in the German Reserves who swore they had no choice but to serve the German Army. The corps screened these men and actually enlisted some of them into our corps. Thinking about this, I realized the terrible position these men were in—they could be shot for treason by either side, if they fell into the wrong hands.

One evening, I sat around a fire with the guys as they passed a bottle of vodka. We all laughed as two men, somewhat drunk; bellowed a song that faded to a discordant hum when they couldn't remember the words.

Still shaking his head, Stefan turned his smile on me. "How about those commandos on San Angelo? They saved our asses."

"Who are those guys, anyway?" I asked.

"They weren't in Siberia," he answered. "They trained together in Scotland. Elite group. Joined us a few months ago. I'm glad they got to us in time." Stefan laughed. "I wonder what the Germans were thinking when they found out we were Poles."

"I bet they never thought they'd see us again," Zbyszek chimed in.

His comment sounded more than rhetorical. I looked at Zbyszek and realized that, like Jozef, he had been a soldier in the army of 1939, when the Germans crushed Poland in a matter of weeks.

"How is this different from the campaign of '39?" I asked him.

"It was totally different then," he said. "First of all, in '39, their sheer number overwhelmed us, but it wasn't just a matter of brute strength. Instead of attacking with artillery and infantry, they came in right away with tanks and air support." He paused to light a cigarette. "They disrupted our communication from the very beginning. My company was separated from the others almost immediately. We didn't know where they were and they couldn't contact us."

"Did the calvary charge tanks on horses, like I read about?" I asked.

"That's complete bullshit," said a man named Ryszard, who sat next to Zbyszek. "The Germans made that up—it's propaganda. They wanted the West to think we were not worthy of their support. You see what they were trying to tell the West? 'The Poles are a joke.' It's a convenient excuse for the West as well: 'Poles on horses trying to attack tanks? Why should we support such nonsense?'"

Zbyszek interrupted. "Remember Andrzej, in war, the victor tells the tales. Think about it, Andrzej. How could a man on a horse attack a tank? Ride up and knock on the armor and tell them he's delivering a telegram? And when they open up, throw in a grenade?"

Ryszard nodded. "I guess if you really wanted to, you could ride up and try to cut a fuel hose, but you're not going to win any battles doing that."

Zbyszek chuckled. "The horses only transported the infantry, just as they transported Germans—the Germans use more horses than anyone. Our infantry battalion moved on horses with the machine guns and 37mm Bofors anti-tank guns. Once we were in position, we dismounted and used the same infantry tactics we use now."

"Transport on horses has its advantages," added Ryszard. "You don't see a horse get stuck in the mud, like these trucks."

"But you can't beat these personnel carriers," Zbyszek said to Ryszard.

"Very true."

I decided I'd had enough vodka and it was time to sleep. Tomorrow, I decided, I'd try to get some information on the Eastern Front.

***

"It's bigger than the entire Italian Theater," said one man I asked. The latest developments were not on the Eastern Front, but in the west, where an incredible number of American and British forces had landed in Northern France. Meanwhile, the Soviets pushed the Germans all the way back into Byelorussia. They were not far from the Polish border. This put pressure on the Germans from the east, west, and south.

Some men said this was good for Poland. The Germans and the Soviets would exhaust each other, and our corps could enter Poland from the south as the Germans surrendered. But the men grew progressively more concerned about reports on the Curzon Line.

I didn't even know what it was until Zbyszek explained it to Kaz and me one day in the mess hall.

"Where are you guys from?" he asked.

"The Grodno area," I answered.

"Well then, you better pray like hell the Allies don't give in to the Soviets on this one," he said.

Kaz stopped eating. "What *is* this Curzon Line?"

Zbyszek tried his beans, made a sour face, and reached for the salt. "Let's put it this way," he said as he sprinkled salt liberally over his meal, "if the Allies bow, Grodno and your homes will be on Soviet territory."

"You're too young to remember," Zbyszek's friend, Ryszard, said to Kaz. "The Curzon Line was once proposed during the Russo-Polish War of 1919 as a possible armistice line."

I vaguely remembered that war from history class. We won the war and the line was never accepted.

"It would strip us of all our eastern land," said Zbyszek. "Land that has been Polish for hundreds of years."

"Six hundred years," Ryszard supplied.

"Churchill almost confirmed the concession in a speech he gave to the House of Commons the other day," said Zbyszek.

"Maybe it's just political maneuvering on Churchill's part," Ryszard suggested.

"What about the press? The Western press is all for it too," said Zbyszek.

I turned to Kaz. "Kolyma gold," I said. "Remember what that guy said about the gold they were mining in Kolyma? He said they were using the gold to buy Western influence."

Kaz listened, then quickly turned back to Zbyszek. "What does General Anders say about this?" he asked.

"They don't care what he thinks," said Zbyszek. "He told them it's preposterous, but they don't care. And it's more than just the land. It cuts Poland off from Rumanian oil, leaving Poland totally dependent on the Soviet Union." He held out his hand, curled like a claw, and said, "They can hold Poland by the throat."

"Churchill may just be telling the Soviets what they want to hear," said Ryszard.

Zbyszek laughed. "You know," he said, "after Siberia, we should understand the difference between politics and the truth better than anyone."

"In this case," said Ryszard, "the empty promise may not be to us, but to the Soviets."

"Wishful thinking," said Zbyszek as he reached for his coffee.

This made me wonder what Churchill, Roosevelt, and Stalin really agreed to in the Teheran conference, held the year before. Officially, the conference had been held to discuss the formation of a second front against the Germans, but we were beginning to suspect that Churchill and Roosevelt had already made a secret agreement with Stalin on the Polish question. Unfortunately, at that point in time, there was nothing we or anyone in Poland could do. Now, all we knew was that we would be going back to the front.

# Chapter Eleven

The next target was an important port named Ancona, on the Adriatic coast. Our objective was to break through the defenses of what was called the Gothic Line and reach the town of Pescaro. The First Canadian Corps would then follow through with a decisive ground attack. As in Cassino, the Germans had fortified their position well, with support from tanks and artillery. The plan was similar to the one executed in Cassino: outflank the Germans from the rear and cut off their defensive position. This maneuver was becoming Anders' signature.

The operation began with an initial attack on Loreto, on the bank of the Musone. Taking Loreto would give us a foothold in the high elevations that could then be used as a springboard for the attack on Ancona itself. My brigade wasn't involved.

Both sides stubbornly refused to give. In contrast to Cassino, modern weapons were of greater value than sheer numbers, and the tank support proved invaluable. Both sides relied heavily on their artillery. The infantry was held off, away to one side.

After several days, we received the order to attack Monte della Crescia.

The attack started with heavy shelling. The Germans countered with their 105mm howitzers. These were heavy guns that fired shells at high angles to reach targets behind cover. My company was assigned a hill to take, and we moved out. Shortly after we started out, we found one of our companies pinned down in the woods. We called in the position to the commander, and waited for the artillery and machine gun squads to arrive.

The exchange in fire seemed to go on forever. I'd been crouching in one spot for so long, the muscles in my legs started to cramp. As I shifted, trying to find some relief, I heard a rustle behind me, followed by a thump as Patryk dropped down next to me. He nodded in greeting, then turned his head to listen. Out in the open, some of the wounded men were calling for help.

Patryk jerked his chin in their direction. "What do you think is worse, Andrzej? Freezing to death, or bleeding to death, like them?"

I was saved from answering by the order to move out. With another nod, Patryk rose and jogged forward to his own squad.

The ground in front of me erupted in an explosion so close, I thought my eardrums had been perforated. Dirt and something else—something warm and wet—rained down on me. I looked down at myself. I was covered with blood.

*Hit! I've been hit!* my mind screamed, but I felt no pain. What was happening? I fell to my knees and felt my stomach and chest; my hands came away slick with blood—the blood was everywhere. But from *where?* My heart pounded like a drum in my ears; I swayed, dizzy, still desperately probing my body for a wound. There was no pain! How could I find the wound if there wasn't any pain? I threw down my rifle, something I'd been taught never to do, and felt my neck and arms. I rose, testing my legs—they moved, bent, supported my weight.

As I leaned over and reached for my rifle, a fat black gobbet of blood fell on the barrel. It had not come from me; this I knew. I froze, watching more thick drops of blood fall on my rifle and on the ground around it. I looked up, then staggered backward, sobbing in horror.

Hanging in a tree above me, as though it were a rag doll torn apart and thrown there by a child during a tantrum, was the upper half of a man's body. *Shell,* my mind supplied as my eyes traveled over the corpse, perversely unable to tear themselves away; he must have been directly hit by a large shell. Finally, my eyes came to rest on the face.

It was Patryk.

\*\*\*

We overwhelmed the enemy with our numbers alone. Monte della Crescia was taken. A day later, the Carpathian Lancers entered Ancona. But rough terrain prevented one

Help

---

brigade from reaching the seashore in time, and the Germans managed to withdraw. Several brigades pursued them and inflicted heavy losses. The soldiers of '39 were clearly on a crusade; over three thousand German soldiers were captured, along with arms and equipment. But our casualties were considerable: almost four hundred dead, including Patryk, and later Mikolaj, from my squad.

I heard that, at the end of this operation, one of the companies from our division captured fifteen German prisoners. They were supposed to bring them back to camp, but someone decided to shoot them all. Two of our colonels investigated the incident. The company claimed the Germans tried to escape; the colonels didn't buy their story, but no charges were filed.

Both our division commander, Lt. General Sulik, and General Anders congratulated us. General Leese, Commander of the British Eighth Army, sent us a letter of congratulations and noted that advancing seventy-five miles up the harsh Adriatic Coast was a commendable feat. George VI, King of England, invited General Anders to a reception, where he offered his congratulations. Anders also received a citation given by President Roosevelt. It read:

> *Wladyslaw Anders, Lieutenant General, Polish Army, for exceptionally meritorious conduct in the performance of outstanding services to the United States and the Allied Nations in Italy from October 1943 to July 1944. As Commanding General of the Second Polish Corps, General Anders brilliantly led his men in the final overwhelming drive that resulted in the retreat of the German Army from the strongly defended Cassino. This point of stubborn resistance was captured when General Anders guided his troops in a coordinated and inspired Allied drive into the bitterly contested vantage point of the enemy. Later, continuing in the eastern sector of Italy on the Adriatic coast, General Anders again led his men in the capture of the important*

*port of Ancona. The outstanding leadership and tactical ability displayed by General Anders were primary contributions to the success of Allied Forces in the Italian campaign.*

*—Franklin D. Roosevelt*

We were very pleased to see the Americans take note of our actions. We were becoming progressively more skeptical of the British and their devotion to a free Poland, particularly with all this talk about the Curzon Line.

\*\*\*

The fighting in this region was over and we were given time to recuperate. Our battalion set up camp in a field not far from a small village in the Ancona region. One Friday night, our squad got passes, and Kaz talked Bogdan and me into walking to the village for a few beers.

The village was relatively well preserved, compared to some of the others. Kaz led us to a café with a certainty that revealed he had been there before. As we entered and sat down, the owner grinned and raised his arms. He yelled something, but the only thing I could make out was "Polacco!"

"Per piacere birra," Kaz said.

The man stared at Kaz for a second and nodded in sudden comprehension. "Birra," he repeated in a very different accent.

We lit Camels and the brews arrived in large, shiny glasses. During our second round, three village girls entered the café. When they saw Kaz, they smiled. As Kaz jumped up and called them over to us, it suddenly occurred to me that Kaz had planned this whole "chance" meeting.

Kaz introduced the three girls as Mariella, Angela, and Laura. They sat down at our table in a flurry of scraping chairs and giggles. There was a moment where we all just sat and smiled at one another, and I grew very self-conscious. I didn't know what to do with my hands. I put both on my lap, realized that looked stiff, and finally wrapped both around my beer.

Kaz took charge. He offered each girl a cigarette. Only Angela accepted. As she lit up, Kaz held up his pack of Camels and said: "Papierosy."

Angela tried to say the Polish word and everyone laughed. "Sigaretta," she said to Kaz.

Kaz tried to say it in Italian and the girls laughed.

Bogdan ordered beers for the girls, something that hadn't even occurred to me. I felt even more uncomfortable. Was there something I should be doing? I had no idea. I took a gulp of my beer, noticed that the girls only sipped theirs, and set my glass back on the table.

The café owner turned on the radio and filled the room with loud music. Kaz asked Angela to dance. He didn't know how to ask her in Italian, so he simply stood up and held his arm out for her. She laughed and followed him. We sat and watched them. Kaz was very animated and Angela seemed to enjoy it. She seemed somewhat theatrical herself. When Kaz made ridiculous motions with his arms and legs, she laughed in delight. Bogdan turned to Mariella, beside him, cocked one brow and held out his arm in invitation. They joined Kaz and Angela.

Laura and I were left at the table alone. We both stared fixedly at the dancers. Every once in a while, I slid my eyes her way, to see if she was looking at me, I suppose. I didn't know what I'd do if she was looking at me—probably whatever I shouldn't do, I thought miserably. I felt paralyzed. I didn't know if she wanted to dance. I didn't ask her.

Kaz and Bogdan showed no sign of returning to the table with their partners. My shoulders were starting to ache with tension. I had to do something. Drawing a deep breath, I leaned forward and offered Laura a cigarette. She declined, but she smiled warmly at me, and I found it wasn't so hard to look at her and smile back. She was pretty. She had black hair curled under in a simple bob, and her light blue dress fit her trim figure perfectly.

I tucked a cigarette in my own mouth, but dropped the matches on the floor. As I leaned over to retrieve them, Angela suddenly screamed like a siren. My head shot up in alarm, banged against the bottom of the table, and I heard a telltale clunk above me as my glass tipped over and spilled beer all over the table. I froze for a horrified moment as Laura jumped up and stared at her dress. I stared at it, too. It looked like one of the targets we used in our maneuvers—one that had been hit by a paint ball.

I didn't know what to do. She snatched a napkin from an adjacent table and tried to dry herself off. *More napkins, you idiot,* I thought, *she needs more napkins!*

I scrambled out from under the table and snatched up more napkins and handed them to her. I pulled the handkerchief out of my pocket and gave that to her, too. "Przepraszam," I said again and again in Polish, but she just stared at me. I didn't know how to say "I'm sorry" in Italian.

Angela and Kaz returned to the table. Kaz scowled at me as Angela helped Laura blot and wipe at her dress. The girls exchanged snippy comments in Italian. I watched hopefully, but the dress looked no better.

"Perdonilo," said Kaz to Laura. It must have meant "I'm sorry."

"Pernilo," I said.

Laura kept muttering in Italian and wiping. She turned and headed for the door. Angela and Mariella followed her to the door, but it sounded like she told the other girls to stay. I approached and indicated that I could take her home.

She shook her head. "Buona notte."

I looked quickly to Kaz. "What is she saying?"

"She said to get lost," said Kaz.

Laura walked out and I just stood there like an idiot. I had no reason to stay myself.

"See you later," I told the guys.

"Don't worry about it," said Bogdan. "Sit down."

"Don't go," said Kaz. "Maybe she'll be back."

I felt too foolish to stay. As I walked out the café's door, I saw Laura almost running down the road. At the same time, I realized that I didn't know the way back to camp. I hesitated, watching Laura, then decided I'd done enough damage for one evening. I turned away.

I hadn't paid attention to the roads as we came into town, but I still reflexively checked the location of the sun, and I remembered where the sun was when we'd been walking. The sun had set, but I could still make out its glow on the horizon. I felt relief when I determined that camp lay in the direction opposite the one Laura had taken, then I felt my cheeks burn with shame. I could face Germans in battle and survive a Russian labor camp, but I couldn't face one girl in a stained dress.

\*\*\*

According to the BBC broadcasts in Polish, the battle in Poland had just begun. The Russians were on eastern Polish soil, while the Germans occupied the remainder of the country.

The Underground army in Poland was controlled by the government-in-exile in London. The exact number was unknown, but estimates put it at 350,000 members throughout Poland, with forty thousand in Warsaw. The highest powers in Britain and the United States knew the Underground's actions and its goals. Since 1941, the Underground army had been resisting the Nazis, but its main purpose was to stage an uprising at the right time. Such an uprising would not succeed without help from outside the country. Unfortunately, the only realistic candidate for such assistance was the Soviet Union. While the exiled Polish government discussed whether the time was right for a general uprising, Soviet radio broadcasts promised support to the Underground army, both in men and supplies, and encouraged them to stage the uprising.

On August 1, 1944, we listened to broadcasts announcing that over forty thousand poorly armed Polish Underground soldiers had attacked the relatively small German force in Warsaw. On the first day, they seized most of Warsaw. We were very anxious about this decision. It appeared the Underground believed the Soviets and counted on the arrival of both Soviet supplies and forces.

"Anders was dead set against an uprising now," said Zbyszek. "I heard he went on record with it."

"I thought you hated generals," said Kaz. "Now you're following what Anders says."

"He's different," said Zbyszek. "Him, I can tolerate."

"Anders may be against it," said Stefan, "but the government in London told them to go ahead and revolt whenever they chose."

"They're crazy to trust the Soviets," I said.

"You have to remember, the people in German-occupied Poland don't know the Soviets the way we do," said Stefan. "They don't know what kind of devil they are dealing with."

"There's no communication," added Zbyszek. "That's the problem. There's no communication between the people in Soviet- and German-held territories. People in German-held land like Warsaw don't know about the camps in Siberia. They don't know the Soviets will screw them at the first opportunity."

"Why haven't we warned them?" I asked.

"How can we?" asked Zbyszek.

"We did," answered Stefan. "But they sent the warnings in the form of cryptic little messages like 'beware of Soviet intentions.' Those don't help. They can't communicate the depth of the Soviet nightmare."

He had labeled the problem correctly; there *was* something nightmarish about this uprising. I could only compare it to watching a movie: the audience might know who the killer was in a crime drama, but there was no way this information could be communicated to the players on the screen.

"You can't expect them to just sit there, occupied, forever," Kaz retorted. "They've organized just for this purpose. The government in London—"

"They're clueless when it comes to the Soviets," Zbyszek interrupted. "The Polish government in London has no idea what the Soviets are like."

"The Underground said they were inspired by our victory at Cassino," said Kaz.

Zbyszek shook his head. "That doesn't mean they should follow our lead. The Soviets will leave them out to dry, I'm sure of it."

"I don't blame them," said Kaz. "If this isn't successful, it's the Allies' fault."

"The Allies won't take the blame," said Zbyszek bitterly. "Politicians are even worse than generals."

We weren't surprised to learn several days later that the Germans sent reinforcements to Warsaw to fight the Underground while the Soviet Army sat in a suburb of Warsaw and watched. The leader of the Underground Army telegraphed London asking for immediate supplies. But in Britain, Field Marshall Sir Alan Brooke refused to use the Polish Parachute Brigade, claiming a shortage of transport aircraft. The American Eighth Army Air Force prepared aircraft to drop equipment for Warsaw but, as we expected, the Soviets refused permission for the aircraft to land at American bases in the Soviet Union. In our camp, men were literally praying at religious services for the Underground, but that was all we could do. We had tanks, artillery, and supplies, but no means of getting them to the Underground.

In the meantime, we had our own battles to fight. In August, with the American Fifth Army, we attacked the Gothic Line in an attempt to drive the enemy over the Metauro River. The German units were strongly supported by heavy artillery, tanks, and anti-tank guns; it turned into a tank battle and our battalion was relegated to patrol. Intensive shelling blinded many of our men. The casualties were in the thousands, but we didn't have an exact figure. When the battle was finally won, we learned it had been our heaviest engagement in the Adriatic sector.

I had always imagined that Americans drove expensive cars, smoked fat cigars, and had lots of money, just like in the movies. But on the Gothic Line, the Americans died like everyone else. I thought they probably had more casualties than anyone.

Despite our casualties, the army got no smaller. We continued to find conscripted Poles among the captured German soldiers. We joked that we were the only army on earth that brought in our reserves from the front and not the rear.

Summer passed, and fall brought heavy rain that turned the terrain to mud. In Warsaw, the uprising continued. Polish pilots based in England had finally started flights to Warsaw in mid-August, but the supplies they dropped were inadequate—the planes had to battle the Germans and not all of them could make their narrow targets. Returning pilots reported a Warsaw in ruins; they'd seen the city burning from over one hundred miles away.

Amazingly, the Underground held out for two months without outside assistance. But on October second, the Germans took prisoner the head of the Underground Army, General Bor-Komorowski, and the uprising ended. The Germans deported the remaining population and destroyed what remained of the city. The Soviet Army still sat in its Warsaw suburb. It was 1939 all over again.

Jerzy, the stenographer, continued showing Stefan Anders' transcripts, and he continued to share them with me. We were particularly interested in the minutes of a meeting between Prime Minister Churchill who, accompanied by General Alexander, met with General Anders during a visit to our headquarters. During the meeting, General Anders expressed concern over losing our eastern territories if the Allies accepted the Curzon Line.

The minutes read, in part:

**General Anders**: *History tells us that some corrections of frontiers occur after each war. I understand that frontiers may be moved ten kilometres to the west or fifteen kilometres to the* *east. But the problem of frontiers should be definitely and exclusively dealt with a peace conference, after the war has been completely finished. But we will never consent to the Bolsheviks, even during the war, taking as much territory as they wish. We will never consent to fait accomplis.*

***Prime Minister Churchill****: Obviously these matters can be settled at a peace conference. (Turning to the General and touching him with his hand): You will be present at the conference. You must trust us. Great Britain entered this war in defence of the principles of your independence, and I can assure you that we will never desert you.*

***General Anders****: Our soldiers have never for one moment lost faith in Great Britain. They know that first of all, Germany must be beaten, and they are ready to carry out any task for this end. This can be confirmed by General Alexander, who knows well that all his orders have always been and will always be carried out. But we cannot trust Russia, knowing her too well, and we are convinced that all Stalin's announcements that he wants a free and strong Poland are lies and impostures. The Bolsheviks want our eastern provinces in order that they may ruin us the more easily and enter more deeply into Europe, to make her Communist. The Russians entering Poland are arresting and deporting our wives and children to Russia as they did in 1939. They disarm the soldiers of our home army, shoot our officers, and imprison members of our civil administration, destroying those who have been fighting the Germans without interruption since 1939. Our wives and children are in Warsaw, but we prefer that they should perish there rather than live under the Bolsheviks. We all prefer to perish fighting rather then to live cringing.*

***Prime Minister Churchill*** *(deeply moved): You should trust Great Britain, who will never abandon you—never. I know the Germans and Russians are destroying your best elements, particularly the intellectuals. I deeply sympathise with you. But be confident, we will not desert you and Poland will be happy.*

\*\*\*

We were withdrawn to the Ancona region to rest. There, I received another letter from Michal. He was nine years old now—I'd missed another one of his birthdays, but vowed I would make it up to him someday.

This letter was similar to the first, but I could see an improvement in his penmanship. He described a club he belonged to that was run by the soldiers of New Zealand. The club was his favorite activity, he wrote. He asked me again if I'd found dad and Stan. I wrote back that I was still looking for them. I knew I would have to tell him about our father someday, but I would tell him in person, not from thousands of miles away.

Food supplies arrived erratically. Some days, we ate like kings, with fresh fried eggs in the morning and steak for dinner. Other times, we had only dry food. When I looked back, I didn't know how I survived the labor camp in Siberia on those measly rations of bread.

A rumor went around that American and British troops had rioted in Ancona. No one knew the specifics, except that it started in a beer hall in an adjacent village and involved several hundred men. We occasionally had our fights, particularly when some of the men got drunk. We almost never fought with the Americans; most fights broke out against the British and occasionally the Australian soldiers. Our commanders did not want us to get into any trouble and they banned us from going to the area.

In October, we were sent off again to a new sector in the Emilian Apennines, where we launched a surprise attack in Monte Grosso. The region was mountainous, with few roads, and we fought a series of slow and tenacious battles rather than one single, large battle. I spent more time on top of Sherman tanks than marching. With every battle, however, we steadily pushed the Germans north.

One day, our platoon was cut off from the rest of the company and its lieutenant. Pinned down in woods at the foot of a cliff by machine gun fire from its top, we had no communication with the others, and by dusk, we still hadn't been relieved.

I realized that the fire wasn't heavy; there couldn't be more than one machine gun squad and one or two infantry platoons up there. If we climbed the cliff when it was full dark, I thought, we could surprise the enemy. The idea was straight out of the manuals I'd read in Iran: *In mountain terrain, surprise attacks can be very successful. Use rough, unlikely routes when visibility is poor.*

I described my plan to the other squad leaders: we could retreat back into the woods and climb the cliff during the night. We were not mountain climbers, but the cliff was not that high, and I could see several small trees in one spot where we could anchor ropes. The only alternative was to totally retreat and then try to find our company.

The squad leaders were skeptical at first, although they did agree that there weren't that many of the enemy up there. As darkness fell, we saw there was no moon; it was a very dark night. The others suddenly saw the merit in my plan.

Slowly, we crept to the foot of the cliff, about two hundred yards to the left of our original position. Several of the men climbed up to the trees and secured ropes, then dropped the coils of rope they'd carried on their backs and continued to the top. The coils unfurled as they plummeted down to the rest of us. Cautiously, stealthily, those of us waiting at the foot climbed to the top of the cliff. It took two hours, but we all reached the top undetected. Once there, we waited for dawn and then skulked toward the Germans' position. The attack must be very quick, I thought; we had no machine gun support and we were out of grenades.

We gave the signal. I was in the lead as we charged into the German camp. We startled two Germans who sat opposite each other, talking. Another stood off to one side, smoking. He wasn't looking our away, but whirled around when our first rifle shot cracked through the air—and went down. We've done it, I thought—we've taken them completely by surprise, this will be a piece of cake. I lifted my rifle, took aim at one of the two seated Germans, and nearly tripped over three more, sleeping in a row at my feet. I turned my rifle on the sleepers and saw the two seated Germans go down from the corner of my eye. More shots pierced the air in quick succession, and the Germans started yelling. Those still standing walked towards us with their arms raised, and the operation was over. The entire operation took no more than ten minutes, and we lost no men.

We'd been right—there were no more than fifty Germans at the top of the cliff. We took seven prisoners.

We held the position until the rest of our company arrived. While we waited, a burning sensation in my right calf that had distracted me earlier grew more insistent, and I noticed my pant leg was torn. I rolled it up to reveal a cut on my calf.

"That's no cut," said the medic who looked at it. "You've been grazed by shrapnel. You're lucky—if it had hit you just an inch to the side, it would have shattered the bone."

I hadn't even felt it happen.

Still preoccupied with that, I brushed aside our captain's praise of my plan to climb the cliff at night. "It was straight out of the manuals," I told him.

We reached the Senio River and the front, which had been constantly shifting, appeared to have stabilized. We settled down for a rest period there, and we received the casualty rates for the Second Polish Corps' operations in the Emilian Apennines: over six hundred dead, nearly three thousand wounded, and thirty-three missing.

I had seen so many dead bodies—on the trains in Siberia, in the Soviet railroad stations, and on the front—that I'd grown inured to their presence. Bodies stacked five feet high were not uncommon after a battle; it was just sad reality.

My attitude towards the dead had changed since Cassino. Then, I would never have considered taking things from dead

soldiers, although I did see others doing just that. Now, I did it
routinely. I did not look for valuables; I strictly adhered to what
my father had told me about greed in war. But I took
ammunition, cigarettes, and chocolate. I considered taking
something valuable, like a gold ring or a coin, bad luck.

After every battle, our attention turned to the events in the
rest of Europe. Germany was being crushed from three sides; it
was just a matter of time before they surrendered. On the
Western Front, the Americans had reached the Rhine River at
Alsace. Both the Russians and Germans were still in Poland, but
the Russians pushed westward, forcing the Germans to retreat
from Polish soil.

Polish Premier Mikolajczyk had been sent to Moscow for
talks with Stalin, Churchill, and Harriman, the American
Ambassador to Moscow. The Allies were putting great pressure
on Poland to accept the Curzon border. This was of special
concern to me; as Zbyszek had explained, if our government
agreed to this, my house, which had been my family's home for
generations, would be in Soviet territory. I didn't want some
Bolshevik commissar in my home.

Stalin was also pushing for the Polish government to be
based on something called the Lublin Committee. I didn't know
what that was, but if Stalin wanted it, it had to be the product of
a Soviet project. The committee members would no doubt be
puppets of Moscow, with no real concern for rebuilding an
independent Poland.

\*\*\*

"It's an unwritten law," said Kaz. "You get promoted, you
celebrate."

I eyed Kaz and Bogdan, who stood over my cot like a couple
of vultures. "Are the girls going to be there?" I asked.

Kaz sidestepped. "We'll have a few beers and some laughs."

"Is Laura going to be there?"

"You know what? She likes you," said Kaz. "Angela told me. Laura likes you."

I could feel heat in my cheeks. "Bullshit," I said. "She likes taking a shower with her clothes on?"

"No, really. Laura wants to see you again."

"I'm busy," I said. I lifted the book off my stomach to show them. "I'm reading."

"It can wait," said Kaz.

"What are you reading, anyway?" asked Bogdan as he turned my book over.

"It's about the French Revolution," I said.

Kaz frowned. "Why are you reading that bullshit?"

"It can wait until tomorrow," said Bogdan. "Come on, get up. Kaz isn't making it up—Laura said she liked you."

"The French Revolution isn't bullshit," I told Kaz. "It's one of the few things Jozef and Patryk agreed about. They both said you can't understand the world today without understanding the French Revolution."

"I know the world stinks, I don't have to know why," Kaz muttered. "Come on. Get up. You're coming with us."

I decided to go with them, but not because of their persuasion. Despite our disastrous first meeting, I wanted to see Laura again. I'd tried and failed to exorcise her pretty face from my mind. Still, I didn't want to appear too eager. "I don't want to face her," I said.

"Just have a beer," Kaz wheedled. "It'll calm you down. Just keep the beer away from her, that's all."

I sat up on the cot. "Is it the same café?"

"No, no, I thought of that," said Kaz. "It's nicer. You'll have a good time."

"How do you say 'I'm sorry about what happened'?"

"Ti amo," said Kaz.

"Ti amo," I repeated, committing the phrase to memory. "Okay. I'll go."

The café Kaz took us to was much nicer—there were even little chandeliers over each table. We each ordered a beer and waited for the girls to arrive. I whispered 'ti amo' to myself every once in a while so I wouldn't forget what to say to Laura when I saw her.

When the girls walked into the café, I rose with Kaz and Bogdan to greet them. My eyes met Laura's and I got mesmerized for a second, then we both laughed. Some of the tension melted from my shoulders. We sat down, and I pointedly pushed my beer away from Laura. She laughed again. I wet my lips in preparation for my apology, but Kaz was trying to explain something to Mariella, and his poor Italian made Angela laugh. When I looked back at Laura, it no longer seemed an appropriate time to apologize.

I recognized Saint Elizabeth of Hungary on the medallion Laura wore on a chain around her neck. Some of the women in the orphanages in Russia and the Middle East had worn similar medallions, and one of them told me that Saint Elizabeth was the patron saint of charities. I looked at Laura and pointed to the medallion. "Saint Elizabeth," I said in Polish.

She looked back at me with her big brown eyes and smiled, but she didn't seem to understand. I wrote the name on a napkin and used the time she spent staring at the napkin to appreciate the smooth curve of her cheek and her long black lashes. I felt an urge to reach out and touch her cheek, but I hadn't yet built up the nerve when she looked up at me, clearly startled that I could identify her medallion. She nodded and smiled.

"Si, si, Elizabeth," she said.

I pointed to her medallion again. I wanted to ask her why she wore the medallion of Saint Elizabeth, but I didn't know how. "Why?" I asked in Polish. She didn't understand. I shook my head in frustration and turned to Kaz. "How do you say 'why' in Italian?"

"Perche," he answered.

"Perche?" I asked Laura, pointing at the medallion.

She answered slowly, but that didn't help me; I had no idea what she said.

"Kaz, listen and tell me what she's saying," I said, and then pantomimed to Laura that I hadn't understood; could she repeat?

Kaz didn't understand what she said either, but he made out the word "sorella."

"It has something to do with her sister," he told me.

I decided to abandon the topic. I smiled lamely at her, she smiled back, and I finished my beer.

I remembered that I still had to tell her I was sorry for spilling beer on her. I turned and looked into her eyes. What beautiful eyes! I frowned in concentration, and tapped my empty glass for emphasis. "Ti amo," I told her.

Kaz's head swung quickly in my direction. Laura just stared at me.

"Ti amo birra," I said.

Laura started to laugh.

Bogdan rose and leaned over the table toward me. He had a big smile on his face. "I think you just told the beer that you love it," he whispered.

My cheeks felt like they were on fire. I jumped to my feet and tried to hit Kaz, but he threw his arms up in defense and laughed. *I'm going to kill Kaz when we get back to the base,* I thought.

"Tell her I meant to say 'I'm sorry about the beer'," I said.

Kaz turned to Laura, thought for a minute, then said, "Desidero chiedere scusa."

I hoped it wasn't another joke, but this time she nodded as though she understood.

I watched Kaz and Bogdan struggling with their Italian for a few minutes. At least they were struggling. I was a basket case with the language. Kaz suggested that we go for a walk, and the girls agreed. Kaz, Bogdan, and I split the bill and left a generous tip, then we all walked out into the cool night air.

Laura slid her hand onto my arm. The move was not passionate, but one of friendly affection. Nevertheless, her touch sent a pleasant shiver up my spine. Her hand looked small and delicate on my arm. I could smell her perfume.

We walked slowly down a cobblestone road, enjoying the pleasant evening and each other's company. I was content with that; it was so much easier just to enjoy Laura's nearness than struggling to communicate.

Angela said something to the other girls, and they spoke together for a few minutes. Then, laughing, Angela and Mariella tugged Kaz and Bogdan down another street, and Laura and I were left alone. We started walking again. I didn't know where we were going, but I was content to let Laura lead the way. She could have walked me up and down every street in the village, and I'd have enjoyed it. She looked up at the clear night sky and pointed at a constellation, then said something to me in Italian. I just smiled.

She stopped in front of a house that I gathered was hers. She said something I didn't understand, but it sounded like "grazie" was in there somewhere.

"Dobranoc," I said.

She said good night in Polish too, and smiled. I hesitated, wanting very much to kiss her, but uncertain how to handle it. In the movies, the hero pulled the woman to him for a passionate kiss, but I didn't think I could pull that off. Laura handled it for me—she leaned forward and kissed me on the cheek. My mouth stretched into what I knew was a silly grin, but I couldn't smooth it from my face.

"I'll see you again," I told her in Polish, but she just looked at me blankly. I didn't know how to tell her so she would understand.

The front door of the house suddenly opened and an older woman stepped out. Her mother? I stepped back reflexively and Laura snapped something to the woman in Italian. I saw she could be abrupt.

I went on my way. It took me a while to get my bearings, but I found the road back to camp. I didn't remember much of the walk back. Once I caught myself touching my cheek where she'd kissed me, and glanced quickly around the deserted road, hoping no one had seen—which made me feel even more foolish.

I reached camp and saw that Kaz and Bogdan were still gone. I lay down on my cot. My head spun gently from the beer and from Laura. *This was the best evening I can ever remember,* I thought, and stretched pleasantly as I brought to mind her warm smile, the softness of her hands and lips, and the heady scent of her perfume, all more intoxicating than beer. This was heaven. I wanted it to go on forever.

I rose, knelt at Kaz's footlocker, and pulled out his Polish-Italian dictionary. The French Revolution would have to wait.

\*\*\*

We woke the next morning to confusion. I heard men yelling outside our tent, and the murmur of conversation and the sound of rapid footsteps. It reminded me of the day I found out about the massacre in the Katyn forest. Kaz and I ran outside to see what was going on.

"Who represented Poland?" a man asked another in a group standing near our tent.

"Nobody, they made the deal between themselves," the other man replied.

"Those bastards! How can they give away a country, just like that?" yelled a private with a rifle in his arms.

"What's going on?" I asked him.

"They sold us down the river," another man grumbled. "Free elections? Free elections under the supervision of the Bolsheviks? Don't make me laugh."

Kaz spotted Zbyszek and signaled for me to follow. "What's this all about?" he asked Zbyszek when we joined him.

"There was a meeting in Yalta between Churchill, Stalin, and Roosevelt," said Zbyszek. "Churchill and Roosevelt have abandoned their support for the Polish government in London."

"What?" I exclaimed. "You mean the Lublin Committee?"

"That's right," Zbyszek said in a grim voice.

"What's this Lublin Committee?" asked Kaz.

"Commies," I told him. "That's the government the Soviets have been pushing for. They've given Poland away to the Bolsheviks."

"The Soviets have promised free elections in Poland," said Zbyszek.

"That's bullshit," I said.

"Of course it's bullshit," said Zbyszek. "But that's what they're saying."

"They decorate us with the Order of the Bath and then give our country away to Bolsheviks?" asked Kaz. "Are these people crazy?"

I shook my head. "What are we fighting for?" I asked.

"This is what happens when you rely on others to watch your interests," said Zbyszek. "You have to take matters into your own hands. But there's more. The territories seized by the Soviet Union are now recognized as part of the Soviet Union."

"You mean the Curzon Line?" asked Kaz. "They went for the Curzon Line?"

In essence, the eastern half of Poland, including the cities of Lwow and Wilno, which had been closely connected with Poland for hundreds of years and had no Russian population, were now Soviet territory. My home, where my great-grandfather was born, was gone. But this was about more than loss of personal property. The loss of the eastern territories meant Poland was completely cut off from Hungary and Rumanian oil. Poland could not be strong without the oil district. The country would be completely at the mercy of the Soviet Union.

"Maybe it's better Jozef didn't live to see this," I heard myself whisper. "This would have killed him anyway."

As we walked around, we heard men saying that they would not fight. I grabbed a flyer I'd seen being passed around and read it. It was from General Anders. In the flyer, he asked us to remain calm. The flyer also contained his letter to General

McCreery, Commander of the British Eighth Army, which
stated:

*We left along our path, which we regarded as our battle
route to Poland, thousands of graves of our comrades in arms.
The soldier of the II Polish Corps, therefore, feels this last
decision of the Three Power Conference to be the gravest
injustice and in complete contradiction to his sense of what is
honorable. This soldier now asks me, what is the object of his
struggle?*

*Today I am unable to answer this question. What has come
about is more than grave; we find ourselves in a situation from
which, so far, I can see no way out... I can see little but the
necessity of relieving those of my troops now in the line, owing
to (a) the feelings of my men as I have described them above,
and (b) the fact that neither I nor my subordinate commanders
feel, in our consciences, the right to demand new sacrifices from
our men.*

*\*\*\**

Jerzy kept us apprised of events at Anders' headquarters.
General McCreery met with General Anders and told him that it
was impossible to withdraw the Second Polish Army, as there
were no replacement units. He emphasized that withdrawal of
our Fifth Division from the sector would have unforeseeable
consequences for the entire British Eighth Army. Both the
British and American military leaders felt terrible about Yalta,
even ashamed, but it was a political matter and there was nothing
they could do about it.

General Anders also met with General Mark Clark of the
American Fifth Army, who told him Yalta was held under
circumstances unfavorable to the Western powers. American
forces were dispersed all over the world, while over a hundred
Russian divisions were heading toward Berlin. "Stalin has the
upper hand," Clark said. But he also added that he doubted if

*Robert Ambros*

Roosevelt would have agreed to this without getting guarantees from the Soviets on Polish sovereignty; after all, he said, there were four million voters in the United States of Polish descent.

General Anders was then summoned to London to meet with Churchill. As before, minutes were made of their conversation, and Jerzy gave us a glimpse of them:

> **Prime Minister Churchill**: *You are not satisfied with the Yalta Conference.*
>
> **General Anders**: *It is not enough to say that I am dissatisfied. I consider that a great calamity has occurred. The Polish nation did not deserve to see matters settled the way they have been, and we who have fought on the Allied side had no reason to expect it. Poland was the first to shed her blood in this war, and sustained terrible losses. She was an ally of Great Britain from the very beginning and throughout the most crucial times. Abroad we made the greatest effort possible in the air, on land and sea, while at home we had a most important resistance movement against the Germans. Our soldiers fought for Poland, fought for the freedom of their country. What can we, their commanders, tell them now? Soviet Russia, until 1941 in close alliance with Germany, now takes half our territory, and in the rest of it she wants to establish her power. We know by experience what her intentions are.*
>
> **Prime Minister Churchill** (*irascibly*): *It is your own fault. For a long time, I advised you to settle frontier matters with Soviet Russia and to surrender the territories east of the Curzon Line. Had you listened to me, the whole matter would now have been different. We have never guaranteed your eastern frontiers. We have enough troops today, and we do not need your help. You can take away your divisions. We shall do without them.*
>
> **General Anders**: *That is not what you said during the last few years. We still want to fight for Poland, free and independent. Russia has no right to our territory, and she never questioned our possession of it. She broke all treaties and*

*grabbed these territories on the strength of an agreement and an alliance with Hitler. There are no Russians in these territories. Apart from Poles, there are only Ukrainians and White Ruthenians. No one asked them to which country they would like to belong.*

So it turned out that this was all the fault of General Anders. I was reminded of what the priest in Buzuluk had said, about making a deal with the devil. Men did what they thought was best under the circumstances, but in the end, only the devil benefited. The Western forces had made a deal with the devil, and now they were giving up the geographic center of Europe to the Bolsheviks.

I had never wondered why the Western powers made an alliance with the Soviet Union until then. I hadn't thought about the priest's comment about dealing with the devil. Why would the West make an alliance with Communist Russia as Bolsheviks and Nazis were killing each other? For the first time, it occurred to me that the Alliance may have been brought about by the influence of leftist forces in Britain and America. I didn't know much about the forces opposing the national doctrine in the Western countries, but I realized they must have been intellectual in nature. These must have been Western idealists who had fallen in love with the concept of equal distribution of wealth and would ignore any Soviet act, however blatantly immoral. It reminded me of what I'd read in the library in Iran—Lenin referred to these Westerners as useful idiots.

It seemed Stalin had learned a trick from Hitler. Prior to the war, Hitler always argued with the Western powers over a small piece of the pie. Once he had them focused on the small piece, and after making certain that an agreement could not be reached; he took the whole pie and claimed that he'd been left with no other choice. Stalin had pretended an interest in the Curzon Line, all the while intending to take all of Poland.

I had always thought General Anders was invincible, but now I saw how helpless he was. We'd been an army in exile;

now we were an army without a nation. It didn't matter to us where they set the new borders of Poland. As far as we were concerned, it was all territory controlled by the Bolsheviks. I swore I would never step foot on territory held by the Soviet Union, as long as I lived. If I discovered Stan was alive and in Poland, I would do everything I could to get him out. Now, I was happy they'd sent Michal to New Zealand.

# Chapter Twelve

Kaz and Bogdan, who was always looking to celebrate, took me out for a few beers for my twenty-first birthday. We joined Laura and her friends in a small café on the outskirts of the village. As it often did in camp these days, our talk turned to what we could do about our situation.

"Seventy, maybe a hundred thousand men against the Red Army?" asked Kaz, shaking his head.

"They're talking about it more and more," I said. "We head north, cross Austria, and enter from the south. We pick up recruits and bring in the government from London."

"We would need the help of the Americans," said Kaz.

I noticed the girls felt ignored. I could tell they were getting annoyed at our protracted conversation in Polish.

My time with Kaz's dictionary was well spent. Although half the time Laura didn't understand me, as the sentence structure was different in Italian, we communicated to the point that I had learned about her family. Laura's sister, Serena, was a missionary. That explained the St. Elizabeth medallion Laura wore—it was a present from Serena. She'd been in Peru for the past five years. When I asked Laura if she wanted to be a missionary, she snapped back that she was not her sister. Once again, I caught a glimpse of Laura's temper.

Laura's father had been the postmaster in the village for many years before suddenly dying from a heart attack; her mother had been the woman who stepped out onto the stoop, the night Laura had kissed me. Laura took care of her mother, who had diabetes, or "sugar," as Laura put it. Laura's mother was known as the best seamstress in the area, but fatigue left her unable to do much work now. Laura supported the two of them by working as a seamstress herself, though her mother also had her husband's pension.

Laura admitted she'd had a boyfriend when I asked her about the ring on her third right finger. He'd joined the army two years ago and had not been heard from since. She didn't want to discuss it, and I saw no reason to press the matter.

Now, I tried to explain Yalta to Laura. I tried to get her to understand that I had no country to return to.

"Non ho paese," I said.

She shook her head.

I tried to tell her Poland was communistic. "La Polonia jest komunistyczna," I said in half-Italian, half-Polish, but she still didn't understand.

"We have no country," I said. "They gave it away to the Communists."

Laura still didn't seem to get it, but Angela started to show some comprehension and she explained it to Laura and Mariella.

Laura turned to me and picked up my beer. "Felicita," she said as she handed it to me. She raised her glass of wine in a toast. I was not sure, but I thought she said, "To happiness."

"Happy?" I asked. "Why should I be happy?"

"One happiness scatters a thousand shadows," she said.

"The only thing to be happy about is that today we are not on the front."

Laura looked away. I realized how bitter I must have sounded, and that Laura had only sought to make me feel better. I reluctantly took a sip of my beer, trying to show her I accepted her toast, but Laura told me she wanted to go. I nodded mutely and followed her out the door.

She set a brisk pace. We walked through the countryside. Neither of us spoke. I reached for her hand, but she pulled it away. We walked for about twenty minutes in an oppressive silence.

A convoy of army trucks filled with soldiers approached, then passed us.

"Poles?" she asked.

"No, Americans. Let them do the fighting," I said. "Why should we? They have a country to fight for. We don't."

"Why don't you just leave the army, then?" she asked.

"Deserto? Non me."

She looked up and gazed impishly into my eyes. "Come on, I can keep you in my house. You can hide in my closet," she said. "You can help me sew to earn your keep, and I'll bring you food. One dress, one loaf of bread. Is it a deal?"

I laughed for the first time in days. I hadn't known she had this goofy side. "Si, si," I said. "Armadio buono."

Her arm slid around my waist. "You can stay there until the war is over. If someone sees you, I'll tell them you're my long-lost brother."

"How will you explain my Italian?"

"That's just it, we'll say you were kidnapped and taken to another country."

"Yes," I said. "Siberia—they took me to Siberia, and now I've come home."

"And I have missed you terribly, Andrei," she added. She held me tighter and turned us toward her street. "Come on, it's time we went home."

She walked us back to her house. I couldn't help wondering if there was some truth to her little joke. At her door, she invited me in, but I declined. Her mother gave me suspicious looks whenever I appeared in front of their house. I kissed her good-bye.

"I guess you will have to stay in Italy then, Andrei," she said.

"We'll see. Buona notte."

***

The Allies wanted to engage us in another operation. At first, the men protested, but General Anders reminded us that the war was not over. "We must continue fighting for the principle that has always motivated us," he said, "right over might." Some men accepted this, others considered it a half-hearted pep talk. But we went on with our duties as if nothing had happened.

We advanced along a highway to Bologna, following the same company of commandos that came to our rescue in Cassino. They'd been expanded into a battalion and underwent special training in cooperation with tanks. They were quite successful in their battles.

They made their way along the Senio River, allowing the Carpathian Brigades to go forward and secure another obstacle, the Santerno River. Our battalion was kept in the rear and didn't come into contact with the enemy until we reached the Gaiano River, where we broke through the defenses and opened the road to Bologna.

The men of '39 had done it again—over two thousand German soldiers were taken prisoner. The commando unit received the "Virtuti Militari," the highest Polish military award. Just two weeks into the operation, we entered Bologna and were greeted by cheering crowds. We did not share in their joy; they were liberated, not us.

That liberation took its toll: over two hundred dead, eleven thousand wounded and seven missing in action. I doubted if anyone would talk the men into another operation after this one. I, for one, did not want to risk my life when an Englishman or an American who had a country to return to could do the same.

To add insult to injury, we learned there'd been a terrible accident at the beginning of the operation. The Americans accidentally bombed the Carpathian Division as they began their offensive, killing over thirty of our soldiers. General Anders had visited the scene of the accident personally, to convince the men to move forward.

Morale was low during our first few days in Bologna, but men's spirits gradually lifted. I had trouble sleeping and could not shake off my fatigue. It was sometimes better not to sleep, when nightmares waited in slumber.

One dream haunted me frequently.  In it, I lay in my cot late at night—past midnight.  I raised my head when someone entered, and saw Michal standing beside my cot.

"Michal, why aren't you in your room?" I asked.  "What are you doing up?"

"Why did you kill Stan?" he asked.

"What?"

"Dad said you killed Stan."

"I didn't kill Stan," I said.  "It was nothing like that at all."

"Dad said Stan was just lying there, resting, and you walked up and shot him."

Horror drove my heartbeat up to a labored tempo.  Why did he say that?  How could I convince him I hadn't killed Stan?

How could I be sure I hadn't?

I sat up on the edge of my cot and gripped Michal by his upper arms, needing to make him understand.  "No, no, no Michal.  That's not what happened.  It wasn't Stan, lying there.  I swear to you that I didn't kill Stan.  I swear to you, I swear to the Almighty, I swear on mom's grave—I didn't kill Stan."

"Then why would dad say that?" asked Michal.

"Dad couldn't have said that," I answered.  "Dad is dead, Michal.  I didn't want to tell you, but he's dead.  The Russians didn't even send him to Siberia.  They tied his hands behind his back and shot him.  They threw his body in a ditch."

I would wake gasping like a man who'd been held underwater, my body wound in my damp sheets.

Kaz knew about the dreams—they often woke him, too.  "Have a few shots before you lie down," he told me, but that didn't help.  The vodka wore off after an hour or two and I was back where I'd started.  Bogdan told me to get some sleeping pills.

"Forget the sleeping pills," said Stefan.  "Maybe you need to talk to a priest."

I pretended not to hear Stefan.  This was none of his business.

*Robert Ambros*

***

Our army was now held in reserve. There would be no more operations, barring the unexpected. The Second Polish Corps had won every single battle it fought with the Germans; the number of our dead and wounded was over seventeen thousand. All to make our way back to a country that no longer existed.

The army was more lenient with us now, and I had ample free time. The weather was good, and I spent the first few days in Bologna drinking beer in the cafés with Kaz and Bogdan.

The city had a medieval character, but many of its impressive buildings had been badly bombed—almost half had been damaged or destroyed. I wanted to find out more about the city, but I didn't know anyone knowledgeable in Bologna's history. When one of the men in my squad told me of a chaplain in our army who had studied in Bologna before the war, I sought him out.

Father Hulewicz was about thirty years old, which was much younger than most of the other priests. I was surprised to see that he smoked. I found him very friendly. He told me he would be happy to give me a tour of the city.

A few mornings later, he led Bogdan and Kaz and me through Bologna's history. I learned that a direct disciple of St. Peter, St. Apollonaris, was the first to teach the Gospel in Bologna. Father Hulewicz told us the city was the scene of many martyrdoms, and the birthplace of many popes. He took us through the cathedral dedicated to St. Peter, which had been rebuilt several times and had multiple altars with numerous paintings by famous masters. The exterior was somewhat damaged, but the interior was magnificent. There was even a cedar crucifix that dated back to the original cathedral, destroyed by fire in 1130.

"It's a tragedy," he said of the bombing that had destroyed some of the magnificent churches. The Church of Corpus Domini, for example, lay in almost total ruins. Before the war, one of the chapels held the mummified body of St. Catherine.

190

The possibility of its destruction seemed to upset Father Hulewicz.

He took us to see famous palaces that had withstood the bombardment and pointed out Rome's influence in the architecture. I saw huge entrance halls, grandiose staircases, and the most beautiful courtyards I had ever seen in my life. "Baroque Period," he informed us.

I gawked like a tourist. *I have to show these courtyards to Laura,* I thought, and imagined here sitting just *there*, on the lip of a fountain.

Kaz was very impressed. "I'd like to stay here," he said. "For university studies, maybe." He arched a querying brow at the priest.

"It's possible," Father Hulewicz told him. "But you must learn the language first. That is the key."

Father Hulewicz wanted to show us more churches. He was energetic and discussed the sites with passion, but we'd had enough for one day. We asked him if he wanted to join us for a beer and, to our surprise, he accepted. But that was exactly what he had: one beer. When we ordered another round he declined, and we sensed he was uncomfortable. We called it a day after the second round and thanked him for the tour.

\*\*\*

"The palaces in Bologna?" asked Laura. "I've seen them." She lay on her stomach with her legs up and happily plucked the petals off a wildflower.

I snuggled in beside her and nuzzled her cheek. "Yes, but you haven't seen them with me. There was one courtyard—"

"Oh, stop," she said, and nudged my shoulder with hers. Her eyes lingered on mine. "You're right, they are beautiful," she said, "but I've *seen* them. There is no need for you to describe each one for me. And there are other places to go—places like this one, where we can sprawl on the grass and talk. Could we do that, in your courtyard?"

She'd let her hair down, and it shone in the sunlight like the wing of a raven. This picnic was her idea, and a very good one. The Italian countryside was very different from my land, but it was just as wonderful.

"If we were in my country," I told her as my eyes lingered on her hair a moment, "I would take you to my favorite spot. It's on our land. Two streams meet at a depression. An enormous fallen oak lies over the point where the streams meet; it's shady and secluded. The water is turbulent, but it's nice and cool, even on the hottest summer day. We would cook fish over a fire instead of having bread, cheese, and wine. I would bring some ale from one of the barrels in my basement."

"I like cheese and wine," she said.

"Oh, don't get me wrong, so do I. This is very nice, too."

She rolled onto her back and examined the few clouds in the sky. "Tell me more about your home," she said.

I sat up and put my arms on my knees. "Well, where I live, there are many forests. Forests, orchards, rivers and lakes, but I like the streams and rivers—I like when water flows. The winters are much colder than they are here. There is a lot of snow, and everyone waits for spring, though I like autumn the best. My family has a fair amount of land—or I should say, we *had* a lot of land—most of it wooded. And we have orchards and fruit and vegetable gardens. There are many streams, and one river flows right through the property. And there are the horses. You can ride—" I realized my words conjured a yearning inside me for a place I would never see again. "Oh, what's the sense in talking about it? It's not my home anymore."

"That's so sad," said Laura softly. "Maybe you'll get it back someday. Still, everything happens for a reason."

I realized that this was the first time I'd talked to someone about my home in a very long time. I hadn't even allowed myself the luxury of thinking about it, but with Laura, it was different. She made me want to remember the good things in my life.

"So tell me about your family, Andrei," she said.

I didn't respond and she picked up on that right away.

"I'm sorry," she quickly whispered.

"Tell me about your sister," I said. "Why did Serena become a missionary?"

"Serena likes to help people. She's always been like that." Laura looked down at her flower. "She's good at it," she said quietly. "She's much more outgoing than me. She's good at showing people how she feels, how she cares."

"What does she do?"

"Everything. She's a midwife, she preaches Christianity to the native Indians, sets up literacy programs—everything." Laura sighed. "Tell me, Andrei, does it make you less of a person, if it's hard for you to let people know how you feel?"

"Of course not," I said.

"Just because it's hard for you to show it, that doesn't mean you don't care."

"No, no, I understand." I reached out and gently touched her soft cheek. She closed her eyes and I leaned over and kissed her. Things felt right. Here, there was no war, there was no Yalta, and there were no Soviets. There was only Laura and the gentle breeze. Laura would be Laura whether we were in the Italian countryside or under the oak tree on my land.

\*\*\*

A story went around camp about a group of Polish political leaders living in London who were invited to Poland by the Soviets to take part in the structuring of the new government. They received official written invitations, including a written statement guaranteeing their safety. Fifteen in all agreed to go, including members of the Polish government-in-exile and leaders of the old army of '39.

They entered Poland and disappeared off the face of the earth. Both the American and British governments inquired about the group, but both Moscow and the Lublin Committee in Poland said they knew nothing of their whereabouts. Then, two months later, the Soviet Union announced that the group had been arrested for diversionary activities against the Red Army.

"They are learning to eat fish head stew in Siberia," someone said.

Even more disturbing, but not surprising to us, was a report that in Poland, the commanders of the Underground Army had been put on trial by the Soviets. They were accused of collaboration with Germany. And this happened less than one year after Churchill stated in the House of Commons that the uprising in Warsaw would never be forgotten. "This epic will be encoded in the memories of the Poles forever," he said. "Freedom-loving people all over the world shall never forget this brave undertaking." These same men, no doubt, were now on their way to Siberia.

Some of the men referred to the British House of Commons as the British House of Empty Promises. After all, it was in these same chambers that Chamberlain declared full support, should Poland be attacked.

Many cursed the British. Chamberlain betrayed our trust in 1939, Churchill supported the Curzon Line, reluctantly agreed to send limited supplies to the Polish Underground during the uprising, and then was himself a key factor in giving away Poland to the Soviets in Yalta.

Others saw it differently. The first uniforms we wore in Uzbekistan were from Britain. As we crossed the border into Iran, we all rejoiced at returning to civilization. In Iran, our meals changed from rice to boiled beef. Orphans and our sick were treated well. Helpless mothers and their children were taken to colonies in Africa, where there was no war. The British gave us state-of-the-art tanks, artillery, and all the ammunition and supplies necessary to fight the Germans.

But some said they supplied us only because it was in their best interest, just as the Soviets let General Anders out of the NKVD jail and treated him well when they realized that they needed his help. This was not a simple issue.

Nonetheless, many of the men, particularly in my division, the Fifth, were more focused on Poland than on Britain. Talk grew of taking matters into our own hands. If a division of Polish soldiers, numbering in the tens of thousands, were to cross Austria and enter Poland with over a thousand armored vehicles and artillery, how would the Soviets react? In actual battle, our division would not have supplies for the long run and could only hold out so long against the Soviets. But some claimed our number would rise tenfold once we entered Poland and took on new recruits. There was also the possibility of raiding Soviet supply depots, once we were in Poland. And how could the Soviets justify the use of force against a bona fide Polish Army? I'd lost my faith in Britain, but I couldn't see how the Americans would stand for it.

General Anders sensed the unrest. We received an order from him that read:

*Men, I am turning to you at a period of extreme difficulty and of far-reaching importance. The Governments of the Western Powers have decided to recognize the so-called Provisional Government of National Unity imposed on Poland by her occupation and thus to withdraw recognition from the legal Government of the Polish Republic in London.*

*It is a heavy blow, the more so in that it is entirely unmerited. For six years, Poland has been unyieldingly engaged in a struggle against the common foe of the Allied Nations. We have suffered enormous losses, and we have offered immense sacrifices on the altar of freedom. We have never allowed ourselves to be seduced by promises and we have not deviated from the road, once chosen. We have kept all our agreements with and obligations towards our Allies and no one can reproach us. The Polish Nation and the Polish soldier boldly look the Allies and the neutrals in the face, conscious that during the war Poland rose to the highest peaks of sacrifice and courage.*

*In spite of this, the fundamental rights of our nation have today been obliterated. The World Powers bypass our* constitution and our lawful authorities, and, in accepting the present circumstances, they have agreed to the fait accompli created with regard to Poland and the Poles by a foreign force.

Men, at this moment we are the only part of the Polish Nation which is able, and has the duty, loudly to voice its will, and just for this reason, we prove today by word and by deed that we are faithful to our oath of allegiance, true to our citizens' duty toward our country, and faithful to the last wish of our fallen comrades in arms, who fought and died for an independent, sovereign and truly free Poland.

This historic role which has befallen the Polish army abroad is indeed a mote in the eyes of our enemies. They will attempt to destroy our Armed forces. We shall all be exposed to their cunning agitation. They will call for our return to our country, but we know all too well how that would end. They will look among Polish soldiers for men of weak resolution. Their work will be easier as a result of the withdrawal of recognition of the lawful Government of the Polish Republic, since the Polish authorities have been deprived of the means of information, even in the form of radio broadcasts from London, which broadcasts have now ceased to serve the cause of Poland.

I do not doubt for a moment that the men of the II Polish Corps, who know why and for what Poland has been fighting for so long, will withstand all hostile attempts. We are one big family, a family born not through any pressure, but born through a mutual devotion to duty for a common cause, and such a family, freely united by bonds of friendship, we desire to remain. Aversion to the use of force still does not mean our submission to annihilation by the enemy. On the contrary, by repulsing such hostile attacks, we will be united and strong.

Men, it is not only today that you have known me. Tens of thousands from among you remember the days we spent together in Soviet Russia. Supported by your faith, conscious of my responsibility, I then sought a way out of an apparently hopeless situation. God blessed my efforts. We found ourselves in a land, foreign but friendly, where we were able to prepare ourselves for *future victorious battles. In these battles along the historic path of Monte Cassino-Ancona-Bologna, our splendid II Polish Corps, marching from one triumph to another, was welded together.*

*The future of the II Polish Corps is assured in these hard days ahead of us. I bear in mind our need for means of livelihood and facilities for further training. I bear in mind not only material issues, those directly associated with us, but also the problems of our families abroad. Whatever may happen, however events may develop, I personally, and all your superior officers, will remain with you and will make the greatest possible effort to safeguard our common achievements, in order to prevent any of them having been in vain and to multiply them for the glory and good of our country.*

*Our country, deprived of the rights of speech, looks towards us. It wishes to see us in the land of our ancestors—to that end we are striving and longing from the bottom of our hearts—but it does not want to see us as slaves of a foreign force: it wants to see us with our banners flying as forerunners of true freedom.*

*As such a return is impossible today, we must wait in closed and disciplined ranks for a favourable change of conditions. This sacrifice must come, or otherwise all the terrible and bloody sacrifices of the whole world, suffered throughout six years, will have been in vain. It is impossible to imagine that humanity has suddenly become blind and has really lost the consciousness of a mortal danger.*

*Men, those who have the unshakable will to fight for life and right, must finally triumph: we read the other day the proclamation of the President of the Polish Republic and the Order of the Day of the Commander-in-Chief of the Polish Armed Forces, both inspired with such faith and will.*

*We will fulfil our duty towards our country and its lawful authorities!*

*Long live the glorious republic of Poland!*
*Wladyslaw Anders, Lieut. Gen.*
*Commander II Polish Corps*

197

\*\*\*

Michal was visiting me in my nightmares again, when loudspeakers suddenly went on and shrieked so loud that I jumped out of my cot as I woke up. I reached for an undershirt and wiped the sweat off my face.

"What's going on?" I heard Kaz mumble.

Someone turned on a light. Everyone in the tent was sitting up. We all knew something had happened; there were never any routine announcements during the night.

"The Germans have surrendered," someone shouted through the loudspeaker. "Repeat, the Germans have surrendered. German representatives have signed an unconditional surrender at Rheims. The war is over."

We just stared at one another, absorbing the news for a moment.

"Said who?" I asked.

"I wonder if they got Hitler?" Kaz mused. He rubbed his hands together and looked around. "So gentlemen, want to celebrate? Anyone got some booze?"

"Celebrate what?" I asked. "Go back to sleep."

\*\*\*

Laura wanted to celebrate the Allied victory and made a surprise visit to see me. I had no pass, but my commander issued me one instantly.

She wanted to head for the festivities in town, and I didn't disagree. "Finally," she said with a broad smile on her face, "no more soldiers have to die." I didn't react and she fell silent.

Music and song echoed amongst the rubble and rose in the squares. Flags from many nations decorated the streets, including the red and white Polish flag. A band marched up and down the streets, but we found the trumpets too loud and slipped down a side street to an outdoor café, where we sat in the bright sun. The waiter who took our order was in a good mood; I suspected he'd had a few.

"You are quiet today," Laura said. "Don't you want to celebrate?"

"Celebrate? Celebrate what?" I asked. I leaned back in my chair and looked away. "Look at them. People dancing and singing. People celebrating what we gave them, and we have none for ourselves."

"Andrei, if you don't want to celebrate the victory, celebrate that I came to see you."

I knew I was spoiling her visit, but I'd been too bitter for too many days to let it go now. "They just used us," I said. "They used us for their own purposes, and then just dumped us."

"At least you will not have to fight anymore," she said.

I looked back at her, and she drew back; I realized I was scowling. "I would not fight, even if they ordered me. Not for the British, anyway."

She sat up straight. She'd stopped smiling. "So this is it? This is your celebration? This is what my visit means to you?"

I let my face, my tense posture, my bitterness melt. "You know I wanted you to come to Bologna."

We paused while the waiter placed a dish in front of me and walked away. I stared at it: a slice of some sort of torte with something green sticking out of it—it looked like a rolled up leaf. I didn't know what it was, and I hadn't ordered it. We looked at each other and laughed.

"Can I ask you about your family?" she asked.

I finally told her about the deportation to Siberia, about Michal, and my search for Stan and my father.

"If they are not in Poland, why do you want to go back?" she asked.

I looked at her. "Who said I want to go back?"

She tilted her head to one side. "If you don't want to go back, why are you so upset about not going back?"

"People belong in their country."

199

"Only if they are happy there," she quickly responded. She looked down at her wine. "You cannot love a country," she whispered, "you can only love people. Even if you went back, if your family is not there, what good is it?"

What she said was true. I only knew where Michal was, and there was virtually no chance that Stan was in Poland.

She leaned forward. "Stay here in Italy. People are good, you will like them. They will like you." She paused. "I like you—very much."

"What am I going to do here?" I asked.

"Have them send Michal back here to Italy," she said. "You can be together and live in Italy."

"He's too young to travel by himself. I'll have to go for him."

She tilted her head back and then nodded as if she knew this was coming. "Soldiers come and go," she said. She sounded resigned.

"What's that supposed to mean?"

She looked away and tapped her fingernails on the tabletop. "If you are leaving, you don't have to explain it to me."

"I'll come back. Besides, I don't know if I'll be going yet. The men may still want to fight."

She looked at me. I saw her temper smoldering in her black eyes. "You don't owe me anything."

"Ritornero," I insisted. "I'll come back."

"Soldiers will say anything," she said. Her eyes fell. "But I thought you were different."

I felt my own temper rising. This was so unfair! "You don't believe I have a brother?"

"I never said that."

"I can show you his letters." I didn't know how to make her believe that I'd come back. I didn't know why I had to.

"You don't owe me anything," she snapped. "Why don't you just tell me you're a Communist and you have to go back to build your new Poland?"

I cursed under my breath and got up to leave, but I couldn't. I stared at the ridiculous looking torte sitting on the table in front of me and finally sat down.

"Vieni con me in Nuova Zelanda," I said.

She laughed, but it wasn't really a laugh. It sounded more like she was clearing her throat to drive the words from her ears. "Me? Go to New Zealand? No, that's impossible," she said, then added, "What do you mean, the men may want to fight?"

"If we get enough support, we may take the Corps into Poland."

"The war is over," Laura said. She crossed her arms and glared at me. "So where are you going? Poland or New Zealand? You can't even come up with one good excuse, so you come of with two lousy ones?"

"I'll eventually have to go to New Zealand for my brother," I said, trying to mollify her. "It's inevitable. He's all I have now."

She looked to one side. I watched her. *Now what?* I wondered, feeling like I was one beat behind in everything she said.

I saw her Adam's apple move as she swallowed. Her eyes glistened when she looked at me. "He's all you have? Then go," she said. "Go to your stupid New Zealand." She stood up and reached for her purse.

"Laura, sit down; I didn't mean it like that."

She ignored me and stalked away from the table. I looked for the waiter but he was nowhere in sight. I dropped some money on the table and trotted after her. I tried to keep pace with her, but she walked rapidly, pretending I wasn't there.

"Perdonami," I said, but she wasn't listening. "Per favore."

Nothing I said affected her. I decided to let her cool off, and walked with her without speaking for several blocks. We came to an intersection but a parade blocked the road, and she had to wait. We watched young children march by, waving colorful flags, for several minutes.

I looked at her from the corner of my eye. She didn't seem as angry as she'd been at the café. "What was that green thing?" I finally asked.

That caught her off guard. She looked at me, eyes wide. "What green thing?"

"In my torte."

She crossed her arms, let her weight rest on one hip, and tilted her head up. "Your brain."

I leaned toward her just long enough to say, "Maybe it was yours." Then I leaned back and smiled.

She sniffed and looked away. "Mine is larger," she said. "My brain knows something good when it sees it."

I sighed. "Then your brain should understand what I have to do."

This was not what I wanted at all. She'd been in a festive mood and I'd taken all the air out of her balloon, but I'd tried to make it up. I may have been a little irritable from lack of sleep, but this scene had gone 'way beyond that.

The flag-waving children passed and the street opened up.

"Where are you going?" I asked.

"None of your business." She stepped into the street.

I tried to hold her arm but she pulled it away. This was even worse than walking to Surgut in the Siberian snow, I thought. At least there, I knew where I was headed. She kept walking and refused to speak to me.

Finally, with a shrug, I gave up and returned to the base.

\*\*\*

A few days later, Stefan, Kaz, and I joined a group of men gathered around the polished jeep of Captain Piotrowski, listening to his recruiting speech.

"Screw the British," said Captain Piotrowski, tough and to the point. "We don't need them." He was another one in the Anders mold. Tall and fit, he had a well-groomed moustache.

He claimed he had the support of thousands of men. "We don't need the British any more than they need us."

"And your commander? He's for it?" I asked.

"Absolutely—he's in charge. We have supplies for a month. The border is only five hundred miles away. We'll be on Polish soil in less than a week."

"You have control over all the division's tanks?" asked Stefan.

"Every armored vehicle is under our command," the captain said, emphasizing his words by jabbing his finger in Stefan's direction. "There are hundreds of tanks, and they're Shermans."

Stefan and I shared a dubious glance. "Will the Americans help us?" I asked.

"They won't even listen to us," he said. "But once we're on Polish soil, it will be different. They'll have no choice but to support us."

"What about intelligence reports? Will they give us reports?"

"Nothing," he said. "But remember, we'll be picking up new recruits as we enter Poland—thousands, if not hundreds of thousands."

"But what does Anders—"

"Spread the word," Piotrowski said. "We're planning to mobilize tomorrow. If you're in, come to our campsite at dawn—the armored brigade base. Spread the word," he repeated, then sat back down and drove off in his jeep.

"He wouldn't talk about Anders," said Kaz.

"He probably didn't want to," said Stefan.

That evening, we discussed the possibility of invading Poland. The atmosphere reminded me of the debate during the blizzard in Siberia, when we'd had to decide what to do. But then, we'd had only minutes in which to make a decision; now, our discussion was more leisurely. We lay on our cots, smoking, and took our time thinking about it.

"I want to get home too," said Stefan, "but with one division? Twenty thousand men? Unless we get the cooperation of the Americans, it's bullshit. They want to raid Soviet supply depots, but we don't even know where those are. We don't know where the Soviet divisions are, and we don't know what propaganda the Soviets have been feeding the people."

"Twenty thousand against the Red Army?" Kaz snorted and shook his head. "Good luck."

"They think the Soviets won't dare shoot at them," said Stefan. "But without help from the Americans, there is nothing to talk about."

"This is our only chance," I argued. "The Soviets haven't established themselves in Poland—they're still recovering from the Germans."

"Twenty thousand men?" Stefan repeated, as if that said it all.

"You don't believe we'll pick up more men once we cross the border?" I asked.

"What are you going to do with them?" asked Stefan. "No training, no ammo—they'll be useless."

"We have ammo," I said, propping myself up on my elbows to look at him. "The new recruits will know where the Soviet bases are, where the supply depots are, and don't forget about the Poles in the Red Army. You don't think they'll join us?"

"You'll end up in Siberia again," said Kaz.

"Not this time," I declared. "This time, I kill them or they kill me. But I'm not going back to Siberia."

"So you do expect them to resist?" asked Stefan.

I shrugged. "We'll see."

"Stefan lay on his cot and stared thoughtfully at the canvas ceiling. "It's not for me," he said. "Not this time. I don't like it."

Kaz looked from Stefan to me and shook his head. "Neither do I."

I sat up and swung my legs to the floor and leaned forward. "Stefan, you once told me we would have to take Poland back by ourselves," I said. "I remember it well. It was back in Siberia."

"I thought it would be different," said Stefan. "Now... no. No, I don't like the odds." He turned his head and looked at me. "You're going, aren't you."

I didn't answer.

"Think this one over carefully, Andrzej," Stefan said.

I lay back down on my cot and closed my eyes, trying to think it through. I hadn't thought I'd be going alone, out of all of us. Suddenly any decision I made was mine, and mine alone. But I wouldn't be deciding for just me anymore, I realized; now I had both Michal and Laura to consider. Such responsibility left me feeling paralyzed. Should I go to New Zealand for Michal, or fight for my home in Poland?

*Jozef!* I seized upon the thought. What would Jozef do? He would go, of course. He wouldn't even think twice. That house in Grodno is mine, I thought. It's Michal's home; he has a right to grow up in that house. That land had been in my family for hundreds of years. It was up to me to win it back. And Stan— *damn you Stan, where the hell are you?*—if Stan was still alive, he'd return to Poland. That's where I would find him.

I'd take Laura to my family's land, to my home. Or I'd cut down some trees and build us a new house on my family's property. We'd live there with Michal—

Yes, what about Michal? Either way, I'd have to temporarily leave Laura in Italy while I went for him. And if I went to Poland in the morning, who would take care of Michal if something happened to me?

I spent a sleepless night, turning over possibilities in my mind without coming to any satisfactory conclusion; finally I just lay there, staring up at the shadows in the tent's peak, and waited for dawn. I'd go. I wouldn't try to solve anything, I'd just go. I had to try.

When dawn finally arrived, I collected my gear; I put my Lee Enfield on my shoulder, and took a truck to the armored brigade base. Men sat shoulder to shoulder in the truck, some with their gear, others without. We joined thousands of other men who stood along the fencing on one side, or gathered in groups, talking.

On the other side of the base, beyond the tents and buildings, I saw rows and rows of tanks and armored cars. Soldiers loaded supplies onto the vehicles while others watched. Ammunition, crates of food, and canisters of gasoline went onto some of the trucks, while teams of men loaded the disassembled parts of heavy guns onto others.

A captain approached our truck as I got off. "Help with the loading," he said. "We'll organize into units after General Anders arrives."

I felt a thrill of excitement at mention of Anders' name. "We're going, then?" I asked.

He nodded. "They had a meeting last night."

"Who?"

"Everyone. Everyone spoke, rank didn't matter. Men spoke their minds. The consensus was to go north, to Poland."

"But what does General Anders—"

"General Anders will be here in a few minutes. He's going to meet with the commander. Help with the loading."

I helped four others load parts of heavy artillery onto trucks. Two of the men helping me seemed to be having the same conversation I had with Stefan the night before as they moved the barrel of a heavy gun onto the truck.

"Where the hell are we going to get gas?" one asked the other.

"There must be gallons of gasoline somewhere in Poland. We won't find it sitting here," said the other.

"And the Soviets are guarding it. You want gas, you'll have to deal with them."

"So we'll deal with them."

"Without the Americans? It'll be a slaughter. What's wrong with the Americans, anyway? Defenders of freedom, my ass!"

Cooks carried big pots of oatmeal around, feeding the men. After I helped load three trucks, I got myself a bowl. As I stood spooning my breakfast into my mouth, a convoy of jeeps arrived.

I made out General Anders and another top commander. This was only the third time I'd seen Anders; the other two times had been during ceremonies. Men saluted as they rushed him into a tent.

They sat in that tent for what seemed like forever.

"We don't have to listen to Anders," men murmured to one another as we waited. I wondered why they thought they'd have to go against Anders. My earlier excitement faded.

After an hour, General Anders walked out of the tent. Thousands of soldiers stared at him; he looked back at us and saluted. We returned his salute. He got into his jeep and left.

A loudspeaker whined to life. "Attention men," said one of the division's commanders. "General Anders has issued advice after hearing the division's plans to move on Poland."

He paused; we heard paper rustling. He must have been sorting notes he'd made during the meeting.

"General Anders states that we should abandon any plan of entering Poland. First of all, even if new recruits join in Poland, there are inadequate supplies to carry out operations. Second, we can expect no help from the Americans. The deal's been made between the United States and the Soviet Union, and that is that. Third, there is little doubt that the Red Army will oppose us in battle. The other Allies do not intimidate them. In fact, the Soviets probably have spies among us right now, and their leaders will learn of this meeting within hours."

"General Anders thinks any entry into Poland would be a suicide mission. General Anders advises that the men accept that the battle is over. We will live to fight another day. That is all."

Men just stood there and stared. My vision blurred; I blinked rapidly, ashamed, until I saw some of the men wiping their eyes. I did the same. I wasn't standing beside the woodpile in Siberia anymore. This was about more than just me.

The men of our division did not have to listen to General Anders. We could have gotten into our vehicles and headed north. But his opinion could not be ignored. No one wanted to take part in a suicide mission. Slowly and quietly, we dispersed. I got back in the truck and returned to my campsite.

\*\*\*

I started each day with the hope of hearing news that the Lublin Committee government had collapsed, but nothing developed. The British continued to finance our army, including my salary. However, they started putting pressure on us to return to Poland. Although they knew we were strongly anticommunistic, they wanted us to take part in the Polish elections and play a part in the reconstruction of our country. I could not think of any scenario as outrageous as Bolsheviks supervising an election. We didn't know whether the British were naïve, or just pretending to be naïve, to get rid of us. I personally believed they didn't know the Soviets well, or the Bolshevik mentality. It didn't appear that they would force us to go back to Poland, though.

General Anders addressed us. Those of us wishing to apply for repatriation could do so, he stated. However, a special camp had been set up for those wishing to go back, and no one could return without going through the camp and receiving a warning. Almost no one applied; of the more than one hundred thousand soldiers who had been in Siberia, only about three hundred of us applied for repatriation. However, thousands of men who had been added to the army after the end of the war applied to go back to Poland. We warned them what they would be walking into, but they didn't listen. Some had left families behind in Poland, and felt they had no choice.

We weren't surprised to learn that the Polish Provisional Government in Poland announced that the Polish Armed Forces under British command would not be recognized in Poland— they were calling for our units to be dissolved. They saw our existence as a threat; I was sure they would love to see us all back in Siberian labor camps. Meanwhile, Radio Moscow broadcasted to Italy that General Anders and his army were engaged in political activity in Italy, and were attempting to crush the Italian Communist Party. The declarations of Moscow and the new Polish government were obviously a coordinated effort.

The army did what it could for us, under these difficult circumstances. Vocational workshops were offered in carpentry, shoemaking, and tailoring as they tried to prepare us for civilian life. Stefan had been a carpenter before the war, and held his own workshop. Universities in Bologna, Padua, and Rome announced that they would allow hundreds of our soldiers to apply for studies. Kaz applied to the University of Bologna and tried to talk me into doing the same.

The colonel of my battalion told me I was obvious officer material. Had the army returned to a free Poland, he said, he would have advised me to enter a military academy. But under the current circumstances, he recommended I take advantage of the offers made by foreign universities.

Ever since Yalta, shady activity amongst the enlisted men had increased. I noticed that more and more men engaged in smuggling. Gold was big, but other items were smuggled as well, particularly gasoline and olive oil. You couldn't blame them; they had to think of themselves, now. It would cost money to get a family member to safety. Not only did the men have relatives trapped in Poland, but many had left family behind on the trail from the Soviet Union to Italy.

I still wasn't interested in participating in these activities. Kaz turned out to be a poor businessman, too. He spent all of his profits from the gold coins he'd purchased in the cafés, with the girls.

I often thought about Laura but, for some reason, I couldn't bring myself to visit her. Every time I had an opportunity to go to her village, I made up some stupid excuse in my head not to go. Snatches of our past conversations replayed themselves in my head, warped by self-doubt: "Stay in Italy, Andrei. You can help me sew to earn your keep, and I'll bring you food."

Here, I had nothing to offer her. If I could only go back home, I could offer her a home and a vast property with orchards and gardens. Of what use was I to her here? A foreigner, a soldier without a country, with no education or craft. I would not live on her charity.

All I needed to hear was that the Communist government in Poland had collapsed, I thought, and my entire situation would change immediately. A legitimate government would never agree to the Curzon Line. I'd be able to take Laura and Michal home.

\*\*\*

Michal still visited me in nightmares; I feared they would affect how I felt about Michal himself, if they continued to plague me. And I feared what the nightmare said about me.

Finally, I entered the confessional in the camp chapel. Maybe there was something to what Stefan said about talking to a priest. I couldn't sleep, and going to confession never killed anyone, I told myself. Besides, once I left for New Zealand, I would not find a priest who spoke Polish or Italian. Even if I did, I thought, I'd much rather talk to a priest who had been in Siberia; we shared a bond.

He sensed something was wrong right away, and asked me if I had a mortal sin to confess.

"I'm not sure," I said.

"You don't know if you've committed a mortal sin?"

I could tell by his voice that he was much older than me— over fifty, I decided. He breathed with difficulty. It sounded like he had asthma.

"I've killed men."

"In combat, you mean?"

"Yes."

"You have a right to defend your homeland," the priest said.

"It's not that simple," I said.

"They took away your homeland by brute force, and they've committed atrocious acts."

He started to cough. I stared down at my hands, clenched so tightly in my lap that the knuckles were white, and waited for his coughing to subside. Finally he cleared his throat and fell silent. Still I stared down at my hands. I could hear his breath wheezing in and out of his nose in the silence. He was waiting for me to say something, but I didn't want to say it.

"Young man, if there is more you have to get off your chest, do so. Now is your chance," he said.

He wanted me to go to a place I didn't want to go. I felt like running out of the confessional. I felt like going back to the tent and finding Kaz to go and have a beer, to pretend everything was normal. I closed my eyes and drew a deep breath; I heard the air shuddering past my lips. "I killed men who were sleeping," I blurted. "I killed a number of them. Some were just waking up and scrambling around... but the first few were asleep."

"Germans?"

"Yes."

"In the field?" he asked, and coughed again.

I used the noise he made to conceal a labored swallow that I was sure the silence would have amplified, otherwise. "Yes," I said when he fell quiet.

"Were they POWs?"

"No. We took them by surprise, early in the morning. We were cut off from the rest of the company. We could have retreated, but I decided to surprise them by climbing up a cliff at night. I was promoted for it."

My face twisted up, and I had to stop for a moment. The silence stretched while he waited for me to finish. "They never had a chance. They were young—younger than me." The words sounded loud, final, in the oppressive silence.

"Could you have taken them prisoner?" he asked.

"I... I don't think so. It happened so fast—in less than a minute. I shot those just rising and reaching for their guns, but

211

before that, I shot the ones who were sleeping. They were just lying there, and I shot them."

The chaplain cleared his throat but said nothing. I didn't know if he was thinking about what I'd done, or if he was deciding what to say to me. Finally he said, "Only... only you, in your heart, know if you could have taken them prisoner. You must pray that God forgives you for taking human life."

"But I was just doing my job."

"But I sense remorse," he countered.

"I—I don't know." I squeezed my eyes shut, and the memory came clearer. The first two I'd seen had been seated opposite each other; one more stood nearby. Then I'd realized there were others nearer; three of them, sleeping. I saw again the shapes huddled under their blankets, saw again the muzzle of my rifle swing towards them. I shot them without even thinking. Could I have taken them prisoner?

No. I would have been an easy target for someone else, had I not shot them.

"Now that I think about it, no—no, I guess I couldn't take them prisoner. If I held a gun on them, the others would have had time to shoot me." But I didn't feel any better. I just knelt there for a minute. Finally I said lamely, "I just feel bad about the whole thing."

"Young man, war is horrible," the priest said. "But remember, they were the ones wearing the uniforms of hatred, not you. Your uniform represents freedom from tyranny, freedom from nationalism."

"I know, I know," I said, and heard the edge of impatience in my voice. "But they were so young. They didn't look like Nazis; they looked like fresh recruits."

"Evil must be punished," he said.

"They didn't look evil, they looked like kids."

"You cannot look into the souls of each of these men and decide for yourself who should be punished and who should be spared. Their ultimate fate is in the hands of God. You can only react to their uniforms and what those represent. You exercised your duty to your cause."

"Then why do I feel so bad?"

"No sane person wants to take human life," he said. "But they—or their fathers—put them in that position, not you."

"Why did they have to pay?"

"For their fathers' sins, you mean?"

"Yes."

"You did not know these men. You do not know if they were good men or not. All you know is that they were trained for evil, and evil must be punished." He coughed and cleared his throat. "Do you have anything else to confess?"

"No," I said.

"The war is over, young man. Go and live your life. Pray that God may forgive you for taking human life. Pray for all the poor victims of this terrible nightmare."

He was right; the war was over. The only way I could put the nightmare behind me was by getting on with my life.

\*\*\*

The slow-moving train finally chugged to a stop near Laura's village. I disembarked and found my way back to her house.

She was hanging up laundry behind her mother's house. My heart skipped when I saw her. Why had I stayed away for so long? Our argument during the V-Day celebrations seemed hazy and trivial now.

She heard me open the gate, but quickly looked away and pretended I wasn't there. I walked up and handed her a shirt from the basket. She accepted it and pinned it to the clothesline.

"So what do you want?" she asked. She concentrated on hanging the shirt and didn't look at me.

"I came to say I'm sorry for not coming to see you."

Her dark eyes flashed my way before she stooped for another piece of clothing. "Do you have another girl?"

I leaned forward quickly and grabbed the next shirt in the basket just as her hand reached for it. I held onto it, forcing her to look at me. "You know I don't," I said in a low voice when our eyes met.

She straightened and regarded me. Her voice softened. "Then why didn't you come? You haven't come to see me in weeks. I thought maybe you left for Poland."

"No, we thought about it, but we decided it wouldn't work. We don't have enough men," I said slowly, taking the time to let my eyes soak in the sight of her. "I don't know why I haven't come. It's difficult to explain. Let's talk. Let's go to a café."

She didn't answer immediately. Her eyes searched my face. "Let me fix myself up a bit," she finally said and turned away, beckoning me to follow. "Come on in."

The house was modest, clean and orderly, with a small entrance hall and several rooms on the first floor. Laura ran up the stairs and disappeared. Her mother sat in the living room, listening to some sort of quiz show on a large radio placed under the main window. She smiled when she saw me, something she'd never done before.

"Buon pomeriggio," I said and she nodded approvingly, but that was the extent of our conversation.

I sat down and pretended to listen to the scratchy radio. Relief made me rise too quickly when Laura returned. She'd smoothed and tucked the stray wisps of her black hair and changed her dress. I nodded and smiled to her mother and we left for the café.

"I'm glad you didn't go to Poland," she said, keeping her eyes on the cobblestones in the road. "It's better for you here. Italy is a beautiful country."

"Beautiful girls, too," I said, and smiled when she looked quickly up at me.

She returned the smile but quickly asked, "So why haven't you come to see me?"

I looked away, down the road. "I don't know. It's hard to explain. I was hoping…"

"Hoping for what?"

"I was hoping the situation in Poland would change."

"So what made you come today?" she asked. "Is the war over for you now?"

I stopped walking and looked at her. "Yes. Yes, that's it," I said. "The war is over for me. La guerra finito. And I care about you. That's why I'm here." I reached over and took her hand. Her soft fingers slid over my palm and gently wrapped around mine. "And I want to be with you for a very long time."

Her fingers tightened; she smiled. I leaned over to kiss her, then impulsively pulled her to me and wrapped my arms around her in an embrace that would have made Humphrey Bogart proud.

When we broke apart, my eyes strayed to an elderly woman who stood in front of her cottage with her broom, staring at us. "Pay no attention to her," whispered Laura as she pulled me close for another kiss. "Signora Ritoni stares at everyone."

We continued down the road and I tried to gather my thoughts. I didn't know how to tell her what I had to do.

As if reading my thoughts, she asked, "And your brother? Have you decided what you're going to do?"

Half afraid that she'd walk away, I tightened my hand around hers. "Laura, I have to go get him. He's my brother."

She sighed. "I know," she said. "But that's why it won't work, Andrei."

"Why won't it work? What's the big deal?" I said gently. "I get him and I bring him back here."

"So many things may happen. You may want to stay there—he may talk you into it. Someone may talk you into going to England or America. You may meet someone and—"

"Laura, nothing is going to change my plans," I assured her.

She shook her head. When she looked at me, I realized that what I'd seen as stubbornness before looked like fear, now. "I don't want to play the fool, Andrei. I don't like uncertainty like this."

I chuckled. "Uncertainty? Don't tell me about living with uncertainty. I've been living in a hellish uncertainty for the past five years," I said. "This isn't uncertainty."

"You say that now."

I stopped, pulled her around, and stared right into those deep brown eyes. "Laura, I'm certain. I love you—ti amo, Laura. Wait for me, because I love you."

She blinked rapidly. A tear appeared on her cheek, and she quickly wiped it off. "I love you too, Andrei, but—"

"But what?"

"But don't leave me," she whispered.

Another tear escaped. I caressed her cheek and brushed it away with my thumb. "I'm not leaving you. I'm just going on an errand."

"An errand? An errand..." she sighed, and her brows dipped as she tried to absorb the idea.

I took her into my arms and kissed her.

Her cheeks flushed, she suddenly looked around. "Come on, we have to keep moving before we make a scene," she said, but she smiled self-consciously. "It's my village, you know. I have to live here."

We walked for awhile without speaking, then she suddenly laughed. "I told you it was a crazy idea."

"What?"

"Going to Poland. I'm glad the others didn't go for it."

"You never told me you thought it was a crazy idea," I said.

She laughed again. "It *was* crazy. Hey, how about we go to that café where you spilled the beer on me?"

"Sounds good."

"Promise not to spill beer on me today? I'll give you one more chance."

"I guarantee it," I said.

\*\*\*

Weeks and months passed. The British finally gave up trying to persuade us to return to a Bolshevik Poland and announced that the Second Polish Army Corps would be transferred to Britain for demobilization. We would be allowed to enter England—there was no other place for us to go.

Bogdan and Stefan said they would be leaving for England; Bogdan dreamed of going to America. Kaz had been accepted into the university in Bologna and would begin his studies with a language course. General Anders would stay in Italy until all of his men had been evacuated, then head for England, as well.

I made frequent trips to see Laura. One day, I went to the New Zealand Embassy in Rome to get a visa. Even though Laura said she didn't want to go with me, I still hoped she would change her mind, and I asked if they would issue one for Laura, as well. Out of the question, they told me. I was only issued a visa because I was an immediate relative of Michal's; Laura was not. I bought a ticket for a merchant ship to New Zealand via Bombay. I had to make my way to the port at Basra, in Iraq, where I would depart for Bombay.

The morning of my departure arrived. I didn't have much to pack: One change of clothes, my letters from Michal, the Cross of Monte Cassino—a medal acknowledging my participation in that battle—and some British pounds. And then there were the army identification cards I had just been issued. The army was planning for the future, and wanted to keep track of us. The situation in Europe was unstable and could change at any time. *The Americans didn't know the Soviets like we did,* I thought, *but they would soon learn.* Things could get hot. I, for one, would be ready to fight, if they did.

The tent flap was pushed aside and Bogdan entered my tent. He was still smiling, but his voice was serious when he said, "Take care of yourself," and extended his hand.

I said good-bye to him, then sought out Stefan and Kaz. I found them in the mess hall, drinking coffee and smoking. I sat down at their table.

"I'm leaving today," I said. "I just wanted to say good-bye."

"Get yourself some coffee," said Kaz.

"You're leaving already?" asked Stefan when I sat back down.

I looked at him. "Yeah. By the time I get back, you'll be gone. You'll already be in England."

Stefan nodded and looked down at his coffee cup. He was still looking for his family but had yet to hear a word, just as I had not heard anything about Stan. There was nothing we could do but wait and see if they made it out of Siberia.

"Bogdan wants to go to America," said Kaz. "So does Zbyszek."

"They've seen too many American movies," I said. "What will Zbyszek do there, fish?"

"Fish?" asked Stefan.

"He's a fisherman, isn't he?"

Stefan laughed. "He's a brewer. His family has been brewing beer for generations. You know the beer—what's the name?" He frowned, then gave up and shook his head. "You know, it's named after the king."

"Why did you think he was a fisherman?" asked Kaz.

I shrugged. "I don't know. You want to go to England?" I asked Stefan.

"Do I have much choice?" he replied. "Where else can I go? There's no work here." He took a sip of his black coffee. "Did you hear about the priests?" he asked. "They're going back."

"To Poland?"

"Yeah, a number of them," said Stefan.

"They've got their work cut out for them," said Kaz. "Priests and Communists don't mix."

"What do you mean?" I asked.

"Think about it, Andrzej," said Stefan. "Bolsheviks and priests living in the same society? Something has to give."

"Siberia for the priests." Kaz said ominously.

"Maybe not," said Stefan. "Maybe the masses won't allow it. God knows what will happen, but something has to give."

Stefan turned and regarded me. "You were a tough kid, Andrzej—I mean, in the labor camp. Nine out of ten would not have made it, I'm sure of that."

I shook my head. "I wouldn't have made it without Jozef and you; I realize that now."

There'd been so many things I hadn't realized, when I was seventeen. I'd never wondered why nobody stole my food or why I never got the worst jobs. Now, though, I knew that had been no accident. Stefan and Jozef had been protecting me the entire time.

"I saw you grow up right in front of my eyes," Stefan said. "When we were marching through that blizzard, I saw the way you plowed forward. There was no stopping you. You were on a mission. My knee hurt like hell, but you inspired me to keep going."

"I could not have done it without you," I repeated.

"Where are you going after you get your brother?" asked Kaz. "Are you going to England?"

"No, I'm coming back here."

"Do you plan to stay in Italy?" asked Kaz.

"I don't know about staying in Italy long term," I hedged. "I'll have to see."

"If you're coming back to Bologna, make sure you look me up," said Kaz. "Just go to the admissions office and ask them where to look for me. It's near Piazza Maggiore, you know, by the leaning towers."

"Yeah, I know where it is."

"Make sure you let the Liaison Office know where you are," Stefan added. "We can keep in touch. We'll meet again."

I got up to leave. I held out my hand to Stefan, but he tugged me into a bear hug. Tears came to my eyes. Who on earth could possibly understand what we had been through?

"God with you," we said to each other.

I looked at Kaz and he put down his coffee. He got up and shook my hand but quickly pushed me away and said, "Go on, get out of here before they change their minds and send you back to Siberia."

I went.

***

"You can't find your ticket?" asked Laura, watching me wide-eyed as I patted my pockets.

The train platform was almost deserted. Trains had been horribly crowded for weeks after the war ended, but it looked like things had calmed down. I was trying to find my train ticket to Ancona. From there, I'd take a cargo ship to Beirut. But I couldn't even get to Beirut, if I didn't have my train ticket. I knew I put it with my papers, but now it was missing.

She put down her bag. "Let me look." She went through my papers and produced a ticket that had been mixed in with letters from Michal.

"That's my ticket for the ship," I said.

"No, no, that's your train ticket. See, it says treno right here." She tapped the spot on the paper.

"If that's my train ticket, let me make sure I have the ocean ticket." I fumbled through my papers again and finally found that one.

As I looked up, my eyes met Laura's. She had tears in her eyes. I took her hands. "Laura," I said, "I'll be back. I'm going to get my brother and then I will come back. I'm coming back to Italy—to you. I'm not going to England."

She started to cry. I drew her into a hug and she put her head on my shoulder.

"I'm not your old soldier friend," I said.

"What?"

"Your boyfriend who never came back. I'm not like him. I'll write you as soon as I get there. I may even get back before the letter does."

Laura buried her face in my neck, then drew back and looked at me. She brushed her tears away and laughed. "Did you notice my dress, Andrei?" she asked. "It's the one you spilled beer on."

I pulled her to me and held her tightly. "I'll buy you a new one," I said.

"That's not what I meant."

"I know."

I felt her reach for something in her pocket; a moment later, she put something into my hand. "It's for you," she said when I opened my hand and saw a gold medallion. "It's Saint Christopher."

I put it on; we hugged and kissed again.

"Do you have your ticket to get home?" I asked.

"I told you before. Yes, I have it, and my train is in half an hour."

We looked at one another. "Ti manchero," I said.

"I will miss you too," she replied.

"Tornero presto."

"Yes, soon, and I'll be waiting," she said, then swept her hand across one cheek, then the other and quickly looked away. "Are you sure this is the train?"

"It says Ancona right on the car," I said.

"It may be a mistake."

"It's for Ancona." I said.

"Then you get on the train, and I will go. You go in and rest. You have a long trip," she said.

"The next time I see you, it will be at your mother's house, with my brother," I said.

"Is he a brat?" she asked, and laughed at my expression.

"I hope not."

"And the orphanage, you took care of that? They know?"

"It's all taken care of. They're expecting him in Bologna."

"Go, then. Go on." She dragged me to the door of a car. "Get out of here. There's no reason for me to stay any longer. Go inside the train and rest."

We kissed one more time. I watched her turn and walk down the platform. She didn't look back, not even once. *Because she knows,* I thought. She finally believed I'd be back.

I took my things onto the train and found a seat. I lifted the medallion on its chain around my neck and studied it. I knew what it meant. Saint Christopher was the patron saint for travelers.

I closed my eyes as the train huff-huffed out of the station. Over the past few weeks, I'd developed a technique to help me fall asleep. I thought of an early autumn day. I pictured myself lying on the grass in my favorite spot: by the stream under the fallen oak tree. The sun still felt warm, but there was a definite crispness to the air, and the leaves in the trees above were just starting to turn. Geese flew somewhere above the trees; their calls blended with the sound of water hitting the rocks. I'd tucked the end of my fishing pole under my leg, so I'd feel the slightest tug. A few trout and a small stack of wood rested by my side. I waited for Laura, who had gone to collect some asters and to pluck a few honey pears off the trees.

I would start the fire as soon as she returned…

\*\*\*

One of my last actions in Italy was to visit the army Liaison Office and file a listing for a person search. One of thousands; the listing would be broadcast via radio throughout Europe. It would also appear in various publications. It read:

*Andrzej Jan Bartkowski of the Grodno region seeks his brother, Stanislaw Jozef Bartkowski, son of Stanislaw and Maria Bartkowski, born October 7, 1920, deported to the USSR in 1940. Reply to listing 45448.*

# Note from the Author

Though fictional, this work is based on historic facts. Approximately 1.5 million people were deported from eastern Poland to Siberia in World War II, but only several hundred thousand made it out of the Soviet Union alive.

For most deportees, Anders' Army represented the only possible path of escape. But Anders' Army represented more than escape from the Soviet Union; determined to regain their homeland, its soldiers began their training half-starved, with rags on their feet and wooden guns on their shoulders. They developed into one of the most respected fighting units in World War II, winning battle after battle against Germany's finest soldiers. Despite this, the role of Anders' Army was barely mentioned (if mentioned at all) in Western texts printed during the cold war.

It is incredible how few people know this history but this is no accident. A conscious decision was made by the Western powers to assign this history to oblivion. For example, thousands of Poles entered Great Britain immediately after WWII. On arrival, they were told by the British government never to discuss their experiences during the war with the British citizens; letters they wrote were censored. Meanwhile across the ocean, a bill endorsed by General Lee, Commanding General of American Forces in the Mediterranean was introduced in the U.S. Congress. The bill would have given special emigration rights to men General Lee referred to as "these gallant soldiers who can't return to Poland." But the bill was quickly killed by Secretary of State Dean Acheson. Several years prior, the USS Hermitage arrived at a California port with over 700 Polish refugees on board; the arrival was kept secret. The refugees were not allowed to stay on American soil but quickly sent across the Mexican border. This history is also completely ignored by most Western historians.

Why would a story that involved the suffering of over one million individuals be first suppressed by the Western governments and then ignored by Western historians? Let them answer for themselves. But clearly the main reason was the fallacy that the Soviet Union was an ally of the West. How could an ally of Britain and the United States have committed atrocities such as the deportations to Siberia or the Katyn murders? How could the public be told this after the Western Allies had been calling the Soviets "our great Russian Allies?" It is incredible how few people, even historians, know of the existence of Anders' Army. The notable exceptions are the American, Canadian, Indian, Australian, and British World War II veterans who fought in Italy. The truth of the Soviet monster became apparent to the public in Central and Western Europe as the Red Army made its way through Poland to Berlin and committed the biggest mass rape in history. The public of Britain and the United States would have to wait until the blockade of Berlin in 1948 to catch their first glimpse of the monster. What would the Western governments tell their public after the blockade of Berlin? Certainly they would not tell them that they ignored the Polish witnesses.

Incredibly, Anders' Army did not prosecute deserters. Several years after the war, future Prime Minister Harold Macmillan wrote of his first visit to Anders' Army: "I remember chiefly about this visit two things. First, the remarkably high standard of drill, discipline, appearance, and *tenue* of the Polish troops. I had not seen anything to equal it during the campaign, except perhaps (I write as a one-time Guardsman!) in the Brigades of Guards. The second impression was more subtle and more difficult to define. It was an extraordinary sense of romance—not gaiety, exactly, but chivalry, poetry, adventure. It was more than a military formation. It was a crusade."

Harold Macmillan also wrote: "In time, II Corps would come to be recognized as one of the greatest fighting forces of the war." With the exception of their recent rediscovery in a free Poland, the existence of Anders' Army and the men and women who served in it have been all but forgotten.

Left homeless by the betrayal in Yalta, most of the soldiers went to Britain after the war, where they joined a resettlement corps for training to enter the job market. In England and Scotland, they were clearly unwanted heroes amidst a surplus of British veterans, also seeking employment. Anders' Army was not invited to participate in the Grand Victory Parade held in London on June 8, 1946, a celebration in which many countries who fought against Germany participated. In Communist Poland, Anders' Army officially did not exist, and a popular song about them entitled "The Red Poppies of Monte Cassino" was banned.

In postwar Britain, the significance of the Poles' contribution to the war effort was downplayed—not only the contributions of Anders and his men, but those of other Polish outfits, as well. Some claimed the Polish victory in Cassino somehow "didn't count" because the Germans had retreated. Churchill wrote that the Poles placed their flag on Monastery Hill but were not the first ones to ascend the hill.

These bizarre claims were made by prominent politicians despite the words of the commander of the British Eighth Army, General Sir Oliver Leese, who, immediately after the battle of Cassino, told a number of foreign reporters, "I want to tell you the capture of Monte Cassino was entirely an achievement of the Poles. I am glad that you are here on this historic day for Poland." It should be noted that many consider the battle of Cassino the fifth biggest battle of World War II; the victory allowed the Allies to capture their first Axis capital, Rome, and prevented the Germans from moving badly needed troops from Italy to Northern France, where an invasion was imminent.

Studying these events sixty years later, it seems as though the Western Allies abandoned any sense of justice in their decisions concerning Polish matters. But it was too late, the deal with the devil had been made, and the Poles, including Anders' men, were seen only as an irritating reminder of injustices that were best forgotten. One can only wonder whether the Soviet system would have survived the war had the Western Allies not aligned themselves with the Soviets. The Soviet Union eventually collapsed, but "Satan's system" continues to haunt the world with missing nuclear weapons and stockpiles of biological weapons large enough to destroy all of humanity.

Although most of the men of the Second Polish Corps were evacuated to Britain, some returned to a Communist Poland and were promptly arrested. Sadly, some of these men were even sent back to Siberia. Had more of the soldiers yielded to pressure by the British government to return to Poland for "free elections," many brave souls would certainly have perished.

Many who went to England remained there for the rest of their lives. Others emigrated to the United States and Canada. Many led productive lives; some like my father suffered from what is now recognized as post-traumatic stress syndrome.

General Anders lived the rest of his life in England, though he never applied for British citizenship. He considered the Communist government of Poland illegitimate, and himself a Pole in exile. He died in May of 1970 and did not live to see a free Poland. At his request, he was buried with his men at the Polish cemetery in Monte Cassino.

Of the various sources I used in researching this book, the most valuable were the testimonies of members of my family. Both sides of my family served in Anders' Army. In their youth, both my parents were deported from eastern Poland to Siberia. My father, Henry Ambros, was a soldier in Anders' Army (15th Poznanski Lancers Regiment) as well as his older brother, Florian Ambros (Jr.) (7th Polish Horse Artillery Regiment). My mother, Adele Ambros, was one of the many children who followed the army to safety. At one point, she thought her mother was dead and was placed in one of the orphanages in Karshi, Uzbekistan before recognizing her mother in a hospital in Iran.   They were reunited and sent to a British colony in Africa.

While in Poland in 1977, I heard the testimony of another uncle on my father's side of the family, Leon Ambros, who served in Polish forces that remained under Soviet control until the war's end.  These were the men General Anders asked Stalin to release to his command, but Stalin never agreed.   My grandfather, Florian Ambros, was also deported to Siberia and was last seen boarding a train for Iran and freedom in 1942.

I also obtained accounts from my maternal grandmother, Maria Ruta, a widow who led all four of her children from Siberia back to civilization.  Her only son, Mieczyslaw Ruta, also became a soldier in Anders' Army (5$^{th}$ Kresowa Division), after ensuring the safety of his three sisters.  One of mother's sisters, Kazia, also married a soldier: Adam Laskowski of the I Polish Corps.

My most valuable written reference was General Anders' book, *An Army in Exile* (Macmillan, 1949).  General Anders' orders, speeches, and conversations with Churchill, as well as Roosevelt's citation and British Eighth Army commander General Leese's speech are all historical fact, and taken verbatim from this book.  In the book's introduction, Harold Macmillan wrote that no American or Englishman could read the book without feeling a sense of shame.

Other valuable references included Harvey Sarner's work entitled *General Anders and the Soldiers of the Second Polish Corps* (Brunswick Press, 1997), Krystyna Skwarko's *The Invited* (Millwood Press, online edition), Kazimierz Cybulski's *Przerwany bieg zycia* (Norbertinum 2000), Slavomir Rawicz's *The Long Walk* (Lyons Press, 1997), William Shirer's *The Rise and Fall of the Third Reich* (Ballantine Publishing, 1960), Robert Goralski's *World War II Almanac 1931-1945* (Bonanza Books, 1981), Alexander Solzhenitsyn's *One Day in the Life of Ivan Denisovich* (Penguin Putnam, 1993), Norman Davies' *God's Playground* (Columbia University Press, 1984), and *World War II* (Smithmark Publishers, 1989). In the Buzuluk camp, the priest's comparison of totalitarianism to a plague was based in spirit from the epilogue of Fyodor Dostoevsky's *Crime and Punishment*. Scripture from The New Testament was quoted from the King James Version of the Holy Bible.

It should be noted that there were Jewish soldiers in Anders' army. In the Introduction of his book, *General Anders and the Soldiers of the Second Polish Corps*, Sarner notes that Poles have too often offended Jews in storytelling, when comparing their suffering with that of the Jewish people. Sarner proposes that Poles acknowledge that the suffering the Jews experienced is unequaled in history, and then tell their own story, making little or no reference to Jews. In order to avoid any unintentional offense, particularly to the people that suffered the most in World War II, I followed this advice and have made almost no reference to the Jewish people. I have only mentioned the existence of rabbis in Anders' Army, and included a very brief description of the army's presence in Palestine. I will only add that I have come across misinformation on anti-Semitism in Anders' Army. For anyone interested in this topic, I found Sarner's work to be the most comprehensive, by far.

I accessed the following web sites for valuable information:

- the Catholic encyclopedia at www.newadvent.org
- www.british-forces.com
- www.virtuti.com
- www.britannica.com
- U.S. army field manuals at www.adtdl.army.mil
- Calculations on sun and moon risings and settings for Northern Siberia in the winter of 1941 were obtained from a U.S. naval web site at http://www.mach.navy.mil

## About the Author

Robert Ambros is a surgical pathologist and lives with his family in upstate New York.